THE
NEW HUMANITY

Our Destiny

Charol Messenger

New Edition *The New Humanity*
Copyright © 2001 by Charol Messenger
ISBN #   Softcover   0-9719901-0-7
(Xlibris ISBN # 0-7388-1515-2 out of print)

This book was printed in the United States of America.

Proofreading by Mary Brinkopf, Lucy Beckstead, and James Raymond
Cover design by Victoria Wolf, Pixel Point Publishing
Printed by United Graphics, Inc.

Book design and copy editing by Charol Messenger,
The Writing Doctor
CharolM@aol.com
Editor: http://members.aol.com/CharolM
Books: http://members.aol.com/CharolMessenger

To order additional copies of this book, contact:
Messenger Inner Teachings Foundation
303-364-2424
504 Evanston Court, #D
Aurora, Colorado 80011-3414

TESTIMONIALS

"Of all the spiritual authors and texts I have read, Charol Messenger's is the most comforting, readable, and flowing. I just have to say that! As a reader of over 95 books on spirituality and a career of 40+ years (teaching, administering, consulting in adult learning psychology, and mentoring 150 graduate folks through masters programs, both genders, all ages, and diverse cultural backgrounds) ... I am impressed. I like Charol's style and the imagery she conveys. *The New Humanity* has a clarity of notions and perspectives and use of words that reach hearts and create motivation in others to embrace the generic nature of spiritual issues while not creating fear of personal recrimination for considering their inner voices by attending to and/or honoring their spirit's beckoning ... I am pleased and actually honored ... Charol has much to offer all of us."

— John S. Brennan, Assistant Headmaster for Resident Prep School (The St. Paul's School) in Louisiana; faculty member at Northeastern Junior College; Colorado State Director of Adult Education; Founding Dean for Regis University's (Denver) adult degree programs, now named the School for Professional Studies

"*The New Humanity* is fantastic! I could hardly put it down. Charol Messenger has a marvelous way of saying the most profound statements in an easy casual way. This book is needed. It is truly written with spiritual insight. Charol is speaking truthfully and straight forward in a way that anyone can relate to. Her writing is clear, uncluttered, and well put. I cheer her on and will recommend this book to all of my friends."

— Ursula Joy, a Reiki master, Smokey Point, Washington

"Charol Messenger's voice is untainted with ego. Here is a crystal-clear, heart-driven message that will bring you peace. Messenger has delivered the message, now will you accept it? The need for this book is enormous. Timely, profound and wise, it is sure to be a classic, referred to again and again."

— Linda Schiller-Hanna, clairvoyant

"The message contained in *The New Humanity* is wonderfully in alignment with the information we have been receiving. It is prophetic and uplifting."

— Judith Coates, co-author of *Jeshua, The Personal Christ,* Oakbridge University Press

"Hey, Charol, I loved your book. I read it on the way to Taos to visit a friend, then I left it with her to read cause I knew she'd love it. It's an easy read, you are so clear, it says so much. I enjoyed reading it because it was so confirming of all my philosophical beliefs. It enriched my spiritual process. Thank you and many blessings."

— Sandi Bianchi, business communications consultant and adventurer

"A wonderful book! It expresses the essence of some very important concepts and perspectives in a very concise manner . . . If people follow their guidance, as laid out in this book, it will prepare them for whatever unfolds."

— John Hornecker, author of *Cosmic Insights*

"*The New Humanity* is an important piece of work for people to identify themselves by. I am inspired by Charol's sharing of her own journey and find the messages in this book to be profound and enlightening. This is a book that will always hold meaning for those who read it, and it definitely will help guide humanity in its quest for knowledge."

> — Athene Raefiel, clinically certified hypnotherapist, motivational speaker, author, spiritual teacher, author of *Getting to the Heart*

"*The New Humanity* will inspire you to be who you really are—in truth—this very moment. The masks of time and frustration will be lifted and you will view a beautiful, loving, harmonious, serene, and compassionate world that is your heritage."

> — Brother Bob, author of *Please Remind Me I Am the Presence of Love*

"This book is terrific! It's powerful! It is so timely. And it covers everything! I think it is really important for people to read."

> — Karl Klaisle, Sanctuary of Light, Elbert, Colorado

"I started your book on the plane Monday (traveling to Kentucky) and then continued reading it on the return trip. I am almost finished and I like it a lot. If you need any validation, I can attest through my experience that everything you state is accurate. Also, your ideas are very timely. This is the time for people to become aware of their true selves."

> — Don Durrett, author of *Conversations with an Immortal* and *The Spirit Club*

"This book is wonderful!"

> — Robert Alan Silverstein, People for Peace Project, PforPeace@aol.com

To every person who seeks hope and inspiration in this changing world, may you realize the great Self you already are.

CONTENTS

PART II

How We Can Achieve the New Society:
Individually and As a Whole

PART III

Our Heritage and Our Destiny

APPENDIX

ACKNOWLEDGMENTS

JAMES RAYMOND, for your steady and unwavering friendship—allowing me to be me! Also for your wisdom and insightful feedback.

Mom for believing in me. My family for accepting me as I am. My sister Jo for our new friendship.

The many good souls who have stood by me throughout my life; in particular, Marja Pheasant, JoAnn Goldsmith, Matthew Patterson, John Cloonan, Ray Alcott, James Raymond, and Keith Klein.

John Brennan, for your immeasurable kindness and belief in this book's value. All of those friends over the years who have encouraged me in my writing. You have motivated me and gifted me in so many innumerable ways. The many readers online and off for your encouragement and excitement.

Mary Brinkopf, for your sound insight, exceedingly wonderful spirit, and exceptional generosity. Lucy Beckstead, for your clear objectivity and adding a bit more grounding. The Integrity Agency intentional writing critique group for your clarification that my personal stories are important to the reader.

My soul, the angels, and the Divine for their inspiration, inner guidance, and encouragement.

ABOUT THE AUTHOR

IN MUCH the same way that waves ripple out from a pebble thrown into a pond, some result always manifests from every cause.

The angels in my life have been several, a force of inspiration instilling me with determination and faith in the intuition that guides me. Following are some of my personal life stories.

A delicate fragrance of rose potpourri filled the quiet room. I curled beneath the blue-violet afghan and gazed out the bay window at prisms of snow filling the crisp Colorado air and floating softly to blanket the white earth. The resonant dancing lights reached into my soul and embraced me.

Alive, I am, forever.

I felt I could see beyond all boundaries, through all. I flowed with the familiar thoughts streaming into my mind. *Be still*, the inner voice said. *Be still and know that God is in you. Be still.* This mantra echoed in my mind, soothed me, calmed me, stroked away my fears. *Be still. Be still and know that God is in you. Be still.*

Drowsiness overcame me and I drifted into a light afternoon nap. Then in the room with me I saw an iridescent figure. The familiar being took my hand and warmth flowed through me. We lifted beyond this world to a very bright hall and stood before a large double door. It opened and we entered a lovely garden of flowers, singing birds, and flowing fountains.

The being departed, and a tall, ageless, spiritual master stood before me. His brown hair and beard complemented his brown priest's robe of the ancient archetypal order of Melchizedek. His deep brown eyes revealed a quite and mellow nature. He took my hand and we strolled through the garden. His stride implied an inner strength born from much experience. In one life, he had been a great prophet, known as Samuel in the biblical Old Testament. After many lives and inner explorations, he had grown beyond the boundaries of external reality and the struggles of human life. He discovered his true Self when he no longer was bound to his body and ascended beyond Earth into the timeless realms as one of the Unseen, neither masculine nor feminine. Then he remembered he is an oversoul—my oversoul, the being from whom I first came to exist as an independent personality.

Until age thirty, I had journeyed through life without consciously knowing of my oversoul's existence. Yet Samuel had guided me; his feelings had impressed me, and his thoughts had reached into my deepest self, embodying the soul presence into my life.

Samuel and I came to a room of mirrors. "Why have you come?" he asked me.

"I want to know."

"What do you want to know?"

"Whatever you will show me."

As we walked through the room, looking at my many reflections of different incarnations, Samuel said of himself, other ascended masters and angels, "We have little more knowing than you, but we have come far since physical lives. Perhaps our insights and understanding will help you and your friends find an easier way."

"What can I do?" I asked.

"Give. That is all we ask. Let others know that life is not coming to any end. Let them know that they are each a divine aspect of the Universal Life Force. Let them know that beings exist who respect and love them and offer support—on request. Let them know all that we will tell you. Be our messenger. Let us teach through you."

We returned to the garden and, as Samuel departed, a tall slender woman with long midnight black hair approached me. She gazed at me warmly, with love and affection, and a reverence fell over me. Alexandra was the other half of me, my "twin flame," who also originally had come from the oversoul; then we each decided to explore different kinds of reality.

"My gift," she said, "is to give you all you have known and to lift you up. Prepare yourself, my friend. Join me now."

We walked and I listened and learned. I transcended into expanded vision and hope.

"Indeed," said Alexandra, "there is always hope."

We planned my life and I came to remember what I had known about the realms of limitless thought. We traversed the universes and I brought back memories of these sojourns, which I share in this and other books.

"Embrace all, be all," said Alexandra. "Know that your dreams are already fulfilled, even as you give yourself to them."

From the time I was twelve years old, I wanted to be a writer. This desire has been a directing passion all of my life. My fifth-grade teacher, Mrs. Snodgrass, at a country school in the Texas panhandle, was the first person to fan this flame by telling me I could write; so I wrote my first novel (not published). Publishing began with poetry during high school when my sophomore English teacher encouraged me to submit to national anthologies. Since then, I have published many articles, short stories, book reviews, and a lot of poetry—in local and regional newsletters and newspapers, university publications, and national anthologies.

The more profound guiding force in my life, however, has been my deep connection with Spirit. It also began at the age of twelve in a Southern Baptist church in downtown Amarillo, Texas, where my paternal grandmother, with whom I was living, dutifully took me regularly. That was her life gift to me.

I always had a talent for spiritual interpretation, and I never accepted status quo beliefs about the nature of creation and the divine-human connection. Even at twelve, I thought for myself and did not accept other people's opinions as my own. Nevertheless, the church experience and the social ties there gave me a strong foundation for my spiritual connection to God. The first step was a deep devotion to service. I wanted to be a missionary. Then life took over and I and my personality traveled many pathways of experience.

The second phase of my spiritual journey began in 1969 in Charlotte, North Carolina, during the years when I was married. Dave was a good man with whom I lived six-and-one-half years; we never had children. 1969 was halfway through the marriage. Once I awakened to my spiritual path, Dave and I grew apart. When I found the courage, I moved on.

My search for life answers was met with reading my first metaphysical book given to me by the woman I worked for in the advertising department at La Marick Beauty Salon Systems in Charlotte. I thank Dot for starting me on this inner journey of deeply satisfying inner growth. The information imparted in *Edgar Cayce: The Sleeping Prophet,* a biography by Jess Stearn, made sense to me. At last, answers to life's questions! From that point, I read voraciously, including: Jane Roberts, Seth, Ruth Montgomery, all Cayce books, and much more. Like others who enter the spiritual path, I was bottomless when it came to absorbing anything to do with getting in touch with my inner being and discovering who I really was, not just a body or personality.

Six years later, in October 1975, in Colorado Springs, Colorado, came the "awakening." After leaving Dave, I had moved there to be with my estranged immediate family and heal the wounds of the past; they had not raised me, but I had always felt close to my stepmother. A series of extraordinary and life-threatening events triggered my latent psychic abilities in a spontaneous awakening of my "kundalini fire," which is a source of tremendous psychic energy that begins with opening the root chakra or energy center in the etheric body. I was thrust mentally and energetically into a shocking and highly dramatic scenario that involved total psychic bombardment from voices and discarnate beings of all descriptions. Since college, I had not been attending church, about fifteen years. Now I found myself thrust into my own "journey through the wilderness" during which the dark side taunted and tempted me and tried to get me to do crazy things, like to drown myself in the bathtub. The entreaties made apparent sense but a deep inborn resistance and intuition told me otherwise and I refused to acknowledge or obey the dark spirits. Instead, with the innate wisdom of an old warrior soul, I instinctively drew to me the universal light and protection of guardian angels and spirit guides—even though I didn't know they were there. I returned to prayer instinctually and asked for God's guidance and help in this "dark night of my soul." This was the critical turning point of my life and the third phase of my spiritual journey. I and my life were never the same again.

The oppressive spirits receded in the face of the light around and in me, because I would have none of what they offered. I was strong and unflinching and stood bravely in the face of darkness, refusing it and all the temptations offered. This transcending and momentous experience, which lasted several weeks but keyed in during a few hours on October 2, was what many people throughout history and in literature have described as a mystical awakening, such as mentioned by René Descartes. This experience also was the initial onset of merging with my oversoul (soul, higher self) consciousness, which meant bringing it into manifestation in my physical life and personality. In some ways, this was akin to a "walk-in" experience; but, in actuality, it was bringing the awareness, dedication, and wisdom of the total Self into the conscious waking mind where I could learn to invoke it at will, live it with intention, and modify the appetites of the personality to alignment with the divine will for this life.

Over the next seven years, I sought the strength of spiritual groups and individuals, during which time I learned to shut off and control receiving and listening to the inner voice as well as to distinguish the sources of different "voices," which could be: my own subconscious, my soul, angels, ascended masters or teachers, various real beings not in physical form, including discarnate spirits (people who have died, both ordinary and disturbed), as well as thoughts from physical persons in this world or other worlds (extraterrestrials). I was not schizophrenic. Thank God my therapist knew that and believed me! In fact, Ron opened his heart and mind with complete nonbias to hearing and learning whatever information I wished to share. This was a period of spiritual growth for both of us; we taught each other. He taught me that it is okay to tell my truth.

Even at the beginning of this remarkable opening into my whole Self, I was receiving wisdom about the deep mysteries of life throughout the universe. Over the years, with a complete devotion to good and dedication to being of service to humanity, the clarity, wisdom, and innate inner knowing grew stronger. In 1979, I felt prompted from within to begin teaching Higher Self integration, even though previously this had not occurred to me and I had never taught anything. That was the first time in my life that I went with the flow and trusted that somehow I would know what to do. That was the beginning of the fourth phase of my spiritual journey.

As my strong inner connection with my oversoul grew, do did my gift as a voice of the Consciousness—the Light that is in us all. After six-and-one-half years of intense self-work, I spontaneously completed merging with my oversoul consciousness during the seven planet alignment on March 5, 1982 (actually a ten-day process, five days before and five days after the alignment). I learned this after the fact, as I frequently do; I follow my intuition, then later learn that my actions were in alignment with some higher purpose. It is neat!

Two months after this alignment, in May 1982, my oversoul began speaking to me through the inner voice; previously, I had heard only spirit guides. Now they departed from direct influence in my life, because with the oversoul connection there is a direct link to the Divine. Oversoul began dictating three books: integrating Higher Self into physical personality, the angelic kingdom, and the transformational times in which we live. This was the beginning of the fifth phase of my spiritual journey and the beginning of my true service commitment and the purpose of this life.

For the next twelve years, I dedicated my life to service full-time as a spiritual channel of the oversoul consciousness, offering personal counsel and teaching workshops. I continued to be a student of the Universal Mind, because learning is continuous; in fact, about the time we think we know it all, we discover we don't.

In 1985, I was certified as a clear channel of the Spiritual Hierarchy by ascended masters Djwhal Khul (always my spirit teacher) and Vywamus through the Tibetan Foundation in Denver, Colorado; I commuted regularly from Colorado Springs. In 1988, I began working as a Higher Self channel with starseeds and walk-ins (I was both), helping them integrate personality with their soul presence. During the 1980s, I also was actively involved with various groups pursuing healing the earth and/or extraterrestrial communication as well as hosting many metaphysical group functions. These activities were in alignment with two newsletters I published—*Global Citizen,* which circulated internationally; and *Ashtar Beacon/Star Beacon,* with a national circulation.

During the twelve years from 1982 to 1994, my view of my role in life expanded. The information given from oversoul expanded my insight and understanding of human nature. Through consistent deep meditation practice and through studying various teachers such as Jonathan Parker, Richard Bach, and Alice Bailey, I attuned to and bonded even more deeply with my *inner knowing self.*

In 1994, now living in Denver, I spontaneously reached a new pinnacle of inner awareness and clarity. In April of that year, my state contract with the Colorado Department of Highways as a long-term temp secretary ended. I had a severe sinus infection, plus I felt totally disconnected from myself, so

I felt a strong need to heal and regroup. It "occurred" to me then (an intuition) that I could claim unemployment compensation and take the physical and mental rest I needed—so I did.

The next six months were the grandest experience of my life. During that time, I was receiving the modest but regular government paycheck and for the first and only time in my life I gave no thought to money. I totally turned myself over to Spirit, devoting every hour of every day to being at-one with my inner being. Everyday I meditated an average of one to two or more hours. I spent one hundred percent of my time totally immersed in reawakening my oversoul consciousness, so that once again I would feel whole and *alive*.

Seven weeks into this self-imposed and self-directed reintegration process, one day during meditation I began to receive new wisdom from the inner voice. It was so exciting! I hadn't "received" in twelve years. The voice was clear and pristine, and I was in awe at the magical mystery of this unexpected new level of attunement, which had followed a serious but easy commitment to healing my inner feeling of voidness. This spiritual alignment was with the monadic Self, which is the divine source from which the oversoul evolved. So, now I was writing and teaching from a much more pristine level of the higher awareness than ever before. This was the beginning of the sixth phase of my spiritual journey. Also, my sinus infection totally cleared.

This alignment with the creative powers of life filled me with an inner urge to write. Thoughts streamed through me unstoppable from a pure heart. The hours, days, and weeks were exquisitely satisfying and fulfilling. The inner voice, from which I took dictation word by word, spoke in my own point of view because the books were written from my monad—that total and most true and clear aspect of myself, for which I am exceedingly grateful to have contact.

First, I received part of my autobiography, including both the soul and human point of view; this included a complete history of my first incarnation as a human being (*How Many of Us Got Here*), which was a very very long time ago. Next, in thirty days, I wrote a book on living the spiritual path (*Petals of Self-Discovery*); then during the next sixty days, a book on how to communicate with angels (*Wings of Light*); then during the next ninety days, completed by the end of 1994, a book about our emerging new society (*The New Humanity*).

During this six-month period, I was in a continuous exalted state. I was so filled with spiritual wonder that I gave no thought to what I would do next. Today, I try to live with that same aplomb and faith, but it requires a lot more intentional focus to be as accepting. One night, years later, when I had been wondering if these books would ever be published, my inner voice woke me at four a.m. and said, *"Sometimes you just have to believe."* Then I fell back into a sound sleep.

My exalted state shifted only when I once again needed to create money. How to do so just came into my mind. "That's a good idea," I said aloud. I acted on the idea, which was to post flyers at college campuses to do typing and editing. Within two days, I had abundant cash flow. That was the beginning of my current full-time home business of freelance copy editing.

Today, at the beginning of 2000, I feel on the verge of entering the seventh phase of my spiritual journey and wonder where it will take me. I know it will feel good, so I will just follow.

As a writer and teacher, I am in service to the Spiritual Hierarchy, also known as the Great White Brotherhood. This organization of ascended beings guides humanity in our spiritual evolution. The word "white" represents goodness and the light and has nothing to do with race. All races, nationalities, cultures, and religions tap into, in some respect, the goodness of life. In this way, we are all one and have the potential to learn to be kind and tolerant of people who are different from us. We are all *earthborn*.

In this book, I call the inner voice or source of the information *The Mind Within*, because we all have access to it. In other books, I explain how to access the inner voice. In this book, I explain how to use it.

I heard that when Mother Teresa was riding the train and chose to be a nun, she chose a life of service because she knew she had a Hitler in her. We learn to rise above our frailties with a conscious intention. We choose to live from our more clear Self.

Mother Teresa is my mentor for selfless service; I strive to live with as much kindness and compassion as she. I frequently fall short, but I am devoted to spending my life to learning to be the best person I can. I have found that connecting with my spiritual Nature is essential to my well-being. When I do not daily attune to the Divine, I am at the mercy of my emotions, which are always considerably active and close to the surface. When I do daily attune and invoke my divine Nature—through focused deep breathing and regular meditation, with an intention toward balance and peacefulness—I achieve greater emotional harmony. In meditation, I reconnect with the spirit I am, and this resets me for living in balance in the world. I have learned that connection to the spiritual Self is key to overcoming destructive thoughts and feelings. The spiritual Self sees the big picture, more effectively handles issues, then moves on rather than dwell in pity, fear, or negativity.

There are many lighted souls in the world. Mother Teresa, Mahatma Ghandi, the Dalai Lama (my mentor for wise common sense). Authors like Richard Bach (my mentor for spiritual story telling) and Gary Zukav (a mentor for calmness). Actors like Richard Gere (a mentor for living true to self). People like Oprah Winfrey (my mentor for how to speak and live my truth). These people and many others are the evidence of what we all can be, each of us in our own unique way.

The greatest lesson we can learn, I believe, is forgiveness—to see the souls in others beneath their pain and to see conflict as opportunities to rise above our own weakness.

May these words from my soul and forgiving heart offer hope and encouragement to be the wondrous person you are.

— Charol Messenger
January 1, 2000
Denver, Colorado

PREFACE

SOMETHING NEW is happening in the world. People are awakening to their spiritual Selves. The result will be a new civilization.

Part one of *The New Humanity* describes the civilization that is our destiny and the kind of people we will be. Part two defines how we individually can become a new human and contribute to creating the new society, which will not come spontaneously but requires our intentional participation. Part three reveals the origin of the human species as well as our splendid destiny that is soon arriving.

The struggles we experience today, the tensions and stresses, short tempers and anxieties, are the beginning of individual and societal change. Through conflict, we are becoming more aware and sensitive.

Transformation is painful. We like things to be familiar. But change in life is continuous. People change and circumstances change.

Today, we have the added stresses of geological disturbances and forecasts of doom and gloom. Countries and nations are striving for individuality and the right to self-governance. Although times are difficult, the picture will get better. We will eventually learn to manage our emotions.

Wars, atrocities, and illnesses are symptoms of fear. Anger is a symptom of fear. Once we learn not to be afraid of what is inside of us, we learn not to fear what is in the world. Once we learn to love and accept ourselves as human—people who want to do good but make mistakes—we learn to forgive our own mistakes as well as the mistakes of others. We learn to be more tolerant and fair-minded, to live and let live, to honor and respect others.

With individual change is coming a stronger communal awareness. That is a picture of the new society we are creating and entering.

With all of the distresses in the world, sometimes it is difficult to remember or to see the big picture of global improvements. Some examples of positive social change are: concern over the homeless, suffering children, the diseased, the handicapped, the equal rights of all peoples; as well as a preoccupation with health and fitness, the decline in popularity of alcohol and smoking, concern with the well-being of animals and ecological balance.

Whenever social foundations go through a tremendous upheaval, as they are now, even when there is positive change, there is fear; people get caught up in the insecurities of constantly unstable circumstances.

The way to counterbalance our fears is to delve into our spiritual Nature and rediscover safety from within.

This new millennium bodes well for humanity, in spite of continuing disagreements. Violence gradually will become less tolerable to the greater number. This will take time, but it is the direction in which we are moving; because, ultimately, despite our fascination with and enjoyment of excitement, we will realize that true joy comes from our spiritual Selves in alignment with each other. We will no longer choose to harm others. We will choose peace.

This book paints a picture of the future that is our destiny. Also given are specific guidelines for how to live in harmony with ourselves and each other, because although the destiny is certain, we will create it by how we live today. The sooner each of us lives as the harmonious person we want to be, the sooner all of humanity will heal.

As we kindle hope and inspiration in our essence, hope for a brighter and better world, inspiration to live magnificently—equal to each other in our presence—we are becoming more clear about our resonance as human beings. We are beginning to see what life can be, beginning to realize that our place is with each other. This, although fraught with trouble and discouragement, is a path of upward escalation.

Earth and we are changing. It is not an easy change. Many are filled with fear and indecision. Yet changing we are.

As we explore reality by our thoughts, traveling as far as our imaginations can carry us, we find a deeper and more elusive world restlessly pushing and prodding us. We feel compelled and driven. We seek to be still. But the rush of life is so great that often we feel carried away in the wake of it. Fear crowds us, fear engulfs us. Change, crises, and instability are everywhere.

Through divine discontent and a passion to understand, we gravitate toward our longings. For some, this is lust or orgies of the mind. For others, it is of the soul and heart. We creep out of our shell slowly and look around carefully. Our soul beckons us to explore, see, and be. So we test our values and ideals. We ask, What is real? Is this all there is? We search for answers.

We live in a time of uncertainty. Yet it is also a time of renewal. If we will but continue onward, listening to the still soft voice within that guides us, we will realize peace. Peace comes in our ability to let go and accept ourselves. Accepting ourselves leads to accepting others. And that is what will change our world.

A step.
This is it.
We begin.

We are on the threshold of a new world,
embracing our greater Selves,
finishing with visions of hatred,
realizing that our sojourn is
creator-being.

Earth Mother,
you have nursed your babes.
We are restless,
ready to tear away from the comfort of known realms.
Mother, what will become of us?
How will we know?

Child,
we are here,
always you are cared for . . . still.
Life breathes
and we fly.

Shall we venture out of our cocoons?
Shall we know that our agonies are dreams and our hopes
reality yet to be?

Divine essence born within leads us on.
We,
angels kin.

Earth is breaking anew,
and we,
sojourners of restored Identities.

Journeys of life are endless.
Gods walked with us when we first came to be.
We knew the elements.
We lived in peace.
Now we experiment with divine compassion and we tread
        higher thought—reconnecting and remembering.

The cosmos is our being, keeping us in its love,
and we just now are opening ourselves.
We have been blind.

The cosmos is our parent.
"Yet even I," says the unborn seed, "am God."
And so now we birth
and pause to consider.

We are transcending.
The only pain is our umbilical boundaries
of mind and heart.
Until we tear away from the safety of our known realities
and spread our light into the skies of our esteem,

will we be brave enough to believe in who we are ... and
be it?

We came here from the stars.
Earth,
home,
is a stop along the way in our travels from early essence.

Earth Mother,
beloved being,
we now break free from our wombs of indecision.
We leap into our higher will,
blessed.

With the Presence as our counselor,
we are devotees
of our god
our unlimited Selves.
Can we walk boldly and *be*?

Carried no more.
Our Brethren who spoke throughout many lives on Earth
now let us go.
Not for lack of love
but for our own steps into a new cosmic understanding.

Like children
leaving the womb of darkness
crying our first cries of ecstasy,
we are coming into a brighter
more exultant reality —

what we were born to be.

PART I

What the World and We Will Be Like

ATTUNING TO THE
CHANGING WORLD AROUND US

The Flood

MY ENTIRE neighborhood was flooded, except for my half of the duplex. My neighbor's basement was flooded, as well as all of the houses around me. I was living alone, with my miniature schnauzer, Cabra, at the foot of Cheyenne Mountain in Colorado Springs, Colorado. Late one night at eleven p.m., a flash flood warning was given on the TV and we were told to evacuate immediately.

I stopped in the middle of ironing and began running around a bit crazily, grabbing up things to put in the car: computer disks and volumes of manuscripts I had written. As I looked frantically about the room at all of my important stuff, I realized with desperation there was no way I could take everything that really mattered, a lifetime of creative materials I still wished to finish.

At that moment, with sudden clarity and assuredness, I declared, "It just can't be!" I instinctively pulled up into my full height and filled myself with my old-soul warrior presence. My mind cleared. My emotions centered to a dead calm. My thoughts focused and sharpened with laser efficiency. I spun through the room and the entire house diligently, declaring, "It

will not be!" Willfully I moved like a shaman, from a sublimi-
nal soul memory, thrusting my arms upward and outward
room by room, projecting a force-field bubble of white light
around the house, visualizing it in my mind's eye. With the
full splendor of my total being, I willed—in both words and
thoughts—that the waters would travel *around* my home. I
visualized with a clear intention the full area protected.

After commanding the flood waters away, having thor-
oughly walked through the house and all perimeters, thrusting
out the innate cosmic power in all directions, suddenly the
task felt complete. A calm contentment came over me and I
knew the energy was set and that I, my dog, my home, and all
within it were protected. I went back to ironing and watching
television.

The next day, I discovered that my half of the duplex was
the only residence in my entire neighborhood for several
blocks around that didn't get flooded; even my neighbor in
the two-story duplex had a flooded garden-level basement,
while mine was dry.

Another interesting note: When I had visualized the waters going around my home, I had forgotten to include in the
mental picture the little fenced side yard and large heavy
wooden doghouse. Thus, the flood waters wiped out the
fence in several places and moved the dog house fifteen to
twenty feet. But the house and the car in the front gravel
driveway were dry.

The Tornado

I was working in downtown Denver in a highrise office
building as a temp secretary on a long-term assignment. I
could see the far horizon twenty miles north where I had lived
since 1990 with Ray, a good and loving man, in the suburb,

Northglenn. Through the earphones on my Walkman radio, I heard the sudden news warning of a tornado going through Northglenn. I had left my border collie, Che, in the fenced backyard and Cabra in the house. Ray was at his job, and I had taken a bus to work, so I wasn't able to get home easily the forty-five-minute drive to move the dogs to safety.

Then an incredibly strong premonition overwhelmed me. I had never felt anything like it before. A sense of impending and grave danger gripped me. My sweaty palms and short breaths escalated. I couldn't reach Ray who worked at Public Service near the house. The radio warnings continued. Anxiety compressed me. I had to do something. Suddenly it "came" to me to invoke the power of the Universe and call on the angels for protection.

With no thought of how ridiculous I might look, but at least hidden by the gray walls of my private cubicle, I immediately began to invoke the protection and project it in my mind's eye to the site of danger. I prayed to the Universe, to God, the angels, Archangel Michael, whoever might hear me (hoping they were all as real as I believed). I asked for guidance and protection of my dogs, Ray, and the house and all within it. The protection ritual *came* into my mind step by step and I followed it spontaneously, just knowing what to say and do, guided as to what words to command, what images to visualize, and what physical gestures to project to send the protecting energy to the site. Then I left the cubicle for more privacy in the ladies' room where I thrust my arms into the air, commanding aloud powerfully (but with a whispered tone), sending the protecting energy to my home and dogs.

I continued this ritual for about fifteen minutes. It was one p.m. in the afternoon. Then suddenly the task felt complete and a calm contentment came over me. I returned to the cubicle and resumed working with no more real thought on the matter, knowing that I had invoked the forces of the Universe and could do no more. I calmly and confidently released the outcome to the Universe, knowing I had done all I could. I was resolved to any outcome, although I felt clearly all was well.

When I returned home by bus at the end of the work day, indeed my strong premonition proved to be true. During the exact same fifteen minutes I had been inner directed to send the protection, according to the TV news reports the tornado had touched down in my neighborhood. In fact, it swept right *over* my backyard. From the debris and damage—and lack of it—I could see the tornado's path. It had skipped *up* at our west fence, then dipped back down at the east fence, tearing out that fence but not damaging *any* part of our property, including the dog house only three feet away where my border collie had hidden during the disaster. She was soaking wet but unharmed. She came crawling out of the doghouse when I went into the backyard. From the east fence, the tornado had ripped a trail right through the neighbor's back lawn.

Well, I believed in the power then. It indeed had kept the elephants away!

In addition to such exciting examples of using our innate mental power, I have averted potential harm in numerous other kinds of situations, including several potential automobile accidents and threatening persons. The power even works to find lost pets; I brought Cabra, my timid and naive miniature schnauzer, home safely and promptly *five* times over the years. She wandered off at a large park; while she and I trekked in the wilderness; in our neighborhood at three a.m. in the middle of a black rain storm; years later, outside the left-open gate of the fenced common yard in the four-plex where we lived. On at least two of these occasions, my vulnerable little schnauzer had crossed busy intersections during rush hour. She was always brought back soon and un-harmed—always promptly after I sent the protection and asked the angels to look after her. After working a protection ritual (this one also "came" to me the first time) and asking the angels for help, after doing all I could using prayer and psychic projection, I truly let the consequences go. Each time, I genuinely released the outcome to the Universe and the highest good of all, not knowing the destiny. Yet, though I was willing to live with the loss, in each instance, my desire for my dog to still be with me was fulfilled. I shared this tech-nique with twelve others and they retrieved their lost pets, too; except in one instance where the animal had already died. This technique is narrated in its entirety in my book *Wings of Light*.

We are all connected through mind and energy, including the earth and the elements of nature. That is how the natural mental protection works. That is why we can indeed protect ourselves and our loved ones—by using the clearly directed power of our inner mind and inner will.

When we study with a regular discipline and daily apply ourselves to oneness with the Divine, we are ready and pre-pared for any crisis. Intuitively and instinctively we respond without a conscious recollection of how we know what to do. We are fully able to defend our being, environment, and loved ones from circumstances that seem beyond our control. No matter how devastating a circumstance might appear to be, how it affects each person is individual. We definitely can eliminate real danger—because everything is energy and can be directed by mind.

Mental energy is the web of life that ties us all together and to all the elements in life. When we are clear and cen-tered, in a moment of crisis or impending danger all of our learned resolve comes to bear effortlessly and instinctively and, as if we consciously invoked it, we are filled with a *knowing* and inimitable power to dissolve danger—by our focused thoughts and aligned energy presence.

When we live in sync with our higher divine will and we daily practice disciplines of mind and spirit (to manage our emotions and impulses), we take on a mature perception toward the life forces and our connection with them. We become one with them in our intentions toward life. In the midst of storms and natural disasters, without fear and with complete presence, we invoke—without question—our full powerful Stature. Our whole Self knows life, is one with nature, and is aligned with clarity and balance. When our whole Self commands nature, nature obeys; because both are a part of the basic structure of physical existence: energy.

How to Be Safe and
Protect Your Loved Ones

Heed your inner warning. When it comes upon you, respond quickly. If you feel a sense of doom, take *immediate* precaution. You may not know why. You may not know the full answer. But acknowledge the fear that fully embraces you and accordingly protect yourself, your loved ones, and your circumstances.

To command nature in the midst of an impending disaster, intuitively and knowingly decree: "Be gone!" Quickly pull in a cushion of light around you and around all that you set visually within your mind's eye. Describe in that instant all that you perceive as potential danger and *command* it away.

The life force in us—generally felt as tingling, vibrating, chills, shivers, or radiating heat—is just as real as electricity and just as potent. When properly focused—as a shield of impenetrable energy visualized around you as a brilliant white light—this *life force* magnificently can deter such effects as floods, tornadoes, and physical harm from other persons or circumstances.

When attuned to your inner counselor's advice, you can perceive danger as it approaches and sense what lies ahead. You can feel and decipher intuitively the inner resonance warning you about potential harm to you, your loved ones, your pets, your home, your belongings, and other people.

By relinquishing the desire to completely control our lives, we enable ourselves to rely on the inner power to guide us, which is an effective tool of warning before we may have any concrete knowledge of something that is about to happen.

If you receive an *inner signal* of impending danger, alter your actions immediately. Quickly pull in a vortex of light around you. Command that the Universe shield you. Ask the angels for guidance and safekeeping. And be *still*.

The Mind Within says: *"When you are disciplined in the use of the power and of the light, nothing in life can harm you."*

With an attuned and heightened perception, we are able to endure potential hazards with grace and equanimity. In some cases, we are able to forestall danger or an environmental impact, or even keep danger away or prevent a disaster, at least to our own environment.

You can protect yourself by using the focused power of your mind and the natural laws of life. Pull in your innate powerful and extraordinary ability to facilitate an energy shield around you. When you know unequivocally that you are self-empowered, you are able to pull in and exactly apply the powerful and innate laws of life—at any time you need them, in their full array—even though in your normal waking state you may not understand why or how it works.

Mind creates. Mind communicates. Mental energy directed with a clear and sure intention is able to alter even the forces of nature.*

* Charol Messenger is collecting short anecdotal stories for two upcoming books: *Extraordinary Acts of Human Goodness*, and *White Light Stories and Other Amazing True Tales*. Send via email with written permission to CharolM@aol.com—a story that is positive and encouraging about a dangerous situation that is averted by a spiritual power (angels or otherwise) and defies any logical or scientific explanation.

THE ERA WE
ARE NOW ENTERING

THE ERA we are now entering has every possibility of being the most extraordinary since the beginning of human existence. We are in transition from the overbearing premise of, "Only help another if it will help yourself."

We are on the brink of a new society. We are changing our perceptions about reality and altering the way we view life. We are learning to release our fears and inhibitions and to allow healing and expansive attitudes; to invite change and even embrace it.

In a time not far distant—an era of increased compassion—humanity will access the higher wisdoms instantly. Already we are beginning to change emotionally and physically in our personalities and bodies. We are in transition spiritually and mentally. These may not be noticeable at times, because until now we have confused values with social standards and ethics with what is legal and we have not been in sync with the cosmic whole that can direct our every thought.

How can you open your inner awareness and access spiritual understanding and reasoning to eliminate fear and frustration and illuminate the path of life before you? How can you unleash the complete Presence that is within you? How can you be unflinching in the face of disaster?

Honor yourself. Evaluate your inner struggles and beliefs that may have narrowed your experiences of joy. Strive to understand the forces that rule human nature. Give of your heart—in an attuned way—to others who struggle to understand the seeming loss of control over their lives.

Humanity's innate inner knowledge of how all of us are connected gives us the capacity to shift focus from the one to the whole and the ability to envision and link compassionately with every other person and life form, including animals. Society's wounds are but extensions of our individual wounds of the heart and soul. We are able to heal these wounds. We are able to reconstruct our personalities and to function as enlightened and balanced persons. Every person is innately imbued with divine inspiration and inner knowing. Every person has access to the inner resonance—that still small inner voice that prompts and counsels us from within.

When not attuned to our spiritual Nature, the inner voice seems in conflict with our own desires and against what we accept as reality. However, the inner voice is the most illumined aspect of our being. The inner voice is the consciousness we name God. Without the inner voice to guide us, we do not live as our true Self, because the human personality is bound to repeated routine. The inner voice teaches us to imagine, envision, and expand our understanding of what is possible. The inner voice brings us certainty in every circumstance.

With this concept tangible in your life, you connect to your spiritual power, your conscience is open and clear, and you develop inner reasoning and align with your true Self. Through *Mind*—which is all of us—you understand the workings of spiritual law and you realize the strategic plan of the Universal Stream of Consciousness.

When we attach our desires to spiritual concepts, we are

guided into realms that surpass known laws of nature. When you live from your inner light, you are not afraid of any person or situation. You know what is truth and what is not. You change how you experience yourself and relate to others. Your ideas expand. Your mind becomes limitless. Your emotions heal. Your body changes. And your spirit fills with a love for all. These are the elements of the new society we are all creating and becoming.

Humanity is transcending its old patterns of behavior. We are evolving new attitudes and new social actions—one person at a time. Every person who is rising into the Divine Mind and releasing personality to Divine Will is becoming a new human. A new human is kind and tolerant, knows inner strength, and experiences life as an exciting adventure where every unexpected turn is a mystery to be explored.

This state of being is unfolding now in all of humanity—one person at a time. Once the whole of us reaches the concept of the all rather than the one, the fabric of human society will shift to a new level of human existence.

The World As It Will Be

HUMANITY is embarking upon a fortunate time. We are re-aligning our perceptions and attitudes and less often seeing the unpleasant aspects of life as catastrophic. We are learning new and honorable behaviors. We are reforming mentally, realizing that what we concentrate on is what we create and what we attend to mentally and emotionally is the reality we steep ourselves within.

As a whole, humanity will reach a saturation point with anger. We will be filled with a distaste for ugliness and will no longer tolerate anguish. We will treat the odd characteristics of society with remorse and no longer fuel distemper. We will abolish views of titillation over the absurd and improbable.

Once all of humanity are receptive to cooperation and alignment with the highest good of all, we will have constructed a new society—thinkers who admire goodwill and discernment.

Our lives depend on how clearly we define honesty, hope, and peace-loving behaviors. We require devotion to and conscious awareness of every person's reasons, motivations, and anticipations. Once we apply intuitive insight to all of our decisions and actions, that is the society we will create.

Physical laws are a byproduct of our mental and emotional consciousness. Consequently, physical manifestation can be directed mentally, even focused willfully and with intentioned results. Humanity actually will acquire procedures to link with every other person whom we previously found disturbing.

This form of reanalyzing what substantially is important to humanity's continued existence will become a central issue in society. We will be so enamored with goodwill and the balance of opinions that we will disengage ourselves from extreme examples of denial and powerlessness. We will reframe our viewpoints to being active consciously in the wellness process.

Once we realize that we can live in harmony with people who are unlike us, we will change our understanding about the purpose of being human. We will acquire such a scope of wisdom that we will initiate procedures that foster hope, power, and reason. We will keep our thoughts to ourselves, display no arrogance or hostility, reason before acting, amuse ourselves with kindness, live in humor, forgive all errors, live calmly and with tolerance, and reframe our points of view to the whole.

These procedures will guide us into becoming more socially aware. We will learn to reason in balance with other people's needs and desires and not to contemplate only our own willful natures. The possibility of compromise will begin to root in us. We will be sensitive to the positions of others and we will care what happens to them. In the new society, it will be abnormal to be uncaring.

Humanity's innate Nature is to live at-one with all. In fact, that is how the human species will survive. Reanalyzing our attitudes will become imperative as the earth reconstructs, because survival will depend upon each one of us being fully able to reach a state of harmony. Embracing cooperation is how we will enhance our lives.

When we are attuned to the whole of life, we have learned

an essential lesson: to reassess our values and accept newer behaviors—honor and cooperation. When we are renewed by our spiritually-centered Identity, we view life with eagerness rather than fear what might come; we view life as remarkable rather than as placidly boring with its monotonous day-to-day redundancy. When our heart is awakened, serenity infuses us and alters our experiences in life.

In the new society, we will forgive our unknowing nature and reposition our beliefs toward reason. Our senses will fill with hope because we will touch our innate potentiality given to us when we were created by the All That Is. This potentiality will be the crux of the new society.

In the times to come, traits normal in our daily routine will be finer insight, reasoning by love, being humble in the face of Providence's power, and accepting responsibility to embark upon a more holy avenue of personal expression. We will grasp higher reason, focus on grand proportions, and imagine any possible solution to any problem. We will no longer subject others to ridicule. Rather, we will fulfill our own inner Nature by listening to our inner being. Our imagination will unfold in full array and we will bestow blessings upon all people by our kind temperament. We will assess circumstances that fill our heart and direct our actions favorably and without desperation. We will dwell in a serene mind and spirit and contemplate our individual uniqueness. We will visualize the greater spectrum of how our talents may be useful to the whole. We will appreciate our innate sweetness and bring it forth as the nectar of our true disposition.

Sweetness is inherent in us. Sweetness is a fragrance born from spiritual insight. When nurtured, sweetness permeates and vitalizes our life. When we embrace our sweetness, it becomes the mode by which we exist.

When we dwell on caution, we live in fear; when we dwell

on confidence, we live in the clarity of the inner counselor. When we dwell on beliefs of separation and futility, we live in anger and frustration and our choices are abusive and misguided; when we dwell on anger, we live in anger. When we dwell on trust, we create hope and delight; when we dwell on harmony, we create equality and fairness and society is blessed by our demeanor. As we overcome our dissonant traits, we reach outward toward others in kindness.

In the times to come, the criteria by which humanity will be measured is how we relate to each other. Attuned visionary behavior and illumined thinking will be the norm. We will be so devoted to wellness—mentally, physically, and emotionally—that we will be unable to conceptualize any other approach toward people's illnesses and misguided actions. We will perceive them and their circumstances with clarity and understanding. This does not mean we will tolerate antisocial or dangerous behaviors. We will do what we can to help those people, but we will not encourage their integration into society until they are well.

In the new society, we will nurture the whole, because it is the whole that we all are. When a single cell is anticonstructive, it is a danger not only to others but to itself. In the times ahead, we will tolerate no dissonant behaviors. Persons with a vindictive character will be considered a danger to society. Those who learn to perceive becoming a blessing to others will exhibit a change of heart and a change of attitude.

Humanity will recognize that the inner counselor is a personal guide. In the times ahead, we will listen to our inner being and focus within to foster wellness—in ourselves as well as others, such as those who grow up angry and afraid.

Each of us is seeded with goodness and higher perception. When we are not afraid of life's mysteries and we grasp life's challenges with full interest, we acquire inner peace, which establishes the fine being each of us innately is.

Tapping the anguish of our lives is like puncturing an infected sore. Once the discoloration of our spiritual Nature runs clear, our sweetness (as if an angel's touch upon us) exudes from our inner being and heals us like a medication of the gods. Sweetness is a primary instinctual behavior that can saturate us until it becomes our entire perspective on life.

The world as it will be is what we are becoming today.

THE WORLD AS
WE KNOW IT ENDING

WE ARE always adjusting to living by our higher Nature. We are always rekindling how to believe in ourselves and to see ourselves as intelligent and loving. Once we discover our spiritual Self, we are filled with hope, patience, and trust in our capacity to rise above our limitations and failures. Life is not smooth and unobstructed. Once we distinguish the natural difficulties of life from what we believe is the way life should be, we no longer misconstrue what life is or suffer from blind perceptions.

The world is on the brink of change. What matters most is that we individually are changing. As we become accustomed to our inner spiritual power, we no longer feel lost within society. We are better able to resist the temptations that daily bombard us. We better focus our lives through the insights of our spiritual Nature. Nothing that happens is a final force that shapes our personality. We choose what will affect our mood. We use higher reason, which enables us to let go of hatred, anger, judgment, and fear. We learn to forgive and to see all people and circumstances as whole, rather than only by their effect on our personal life.

To see how your life might result from your insights and actions, rekindle the definitive presence of your *inner knowing self* and realize that the world does not cause who you are.

Our personalities respond to life events according to how we see ourselves. As you become alive with hope and perceive our ideal Nature, we infuse ourselves with compassion for the disillusionment that belittles self-esteem.

Daily and ongoing self-initiated karma is the universal natural law of cause and effect, which is a component of all life. When we restyle our attitudes, we are restyling the direction toward which we are evolving both spiritually and in our manifest life. When we support other people's dreams and desires, the more our own conscience instructs us on how to better serve the whole of humanity. The more we strive to live from our true capacity, the more we rise into social consciousness as a standard by which to live.

Society does not delineate our individual character. Rather, each of us delineates the evolution of humanity. What each of us perceives, understands, and applies becomes a part of the character of the whole. The more individuals who believe in living by spiritual compassion and insight—rather than living on the edge according to the perceived status quo—the more this will become the view of all society. Every person is significantly affecting the nature of life, because everything each of us is extends into what humanity becomes. In time, the world will reshape according to our fondest common hopes and dreams.

The evolution of humanity is a composite process. The species will survive and evolve because the greater number of us are filling ourselves with a belief in higher truth; and not defining what that truth must be nor what that truth must look like, just accepting that higher knowledge is a way to learn to live more humanely and with greater satisfaction and fulfillment.

The world is changing because each of us is changing.

What we are is altering. Our attitudes are fluid and in flux. Our beliefs are moving toward the clarity of the precious inner power. Everything we imagine is possible, both good and bad. Therefore, to create a good society, it is essential that we believe in humanity's innate goodness.

Hope is an important commodity. Hope is the sunlight of our souls, a fragrance of divine vision. As we invest in our higher sensitivity, hope predominates in our personality as a guiding principle for all of our beliefs and desires.

How can you change your attitudes to comprehend more easily the fluctuating beliefs and standards of what is right? Believe in your self-worth. Draw conclusions by analyzing other people's strategies and behaviors. Assume that other people can establish their own workable solutions. Establish your own in order to acquire the precious insight.

What does it take to discover the fears that may obscure your perspective? Create a view of life that is aligned with your heart. *Thoughtfully* apprise others of your personal opinions about the actions of society. Assess what matters and what does not. If ever you fear the consequences of your decisions, reevaluate what is important in your life. Create the attitude of living at-one with all persons. When we are able to assess our actions as honorable and nondestructive, we are able to create and foster hope. That is how we manifest the precious inner power.

To be free from dismay, deliver yourself from self-denial. Reacquaint yourself with your innate better Nature. Surround yourself with the higher wisdom from the Unseen Protectors of higher thought. Assume a new impression of how to attest to *this* new vision: that humanity is transcending its patterns of thought and someday the old ways of life no longer will be important to us.

To reassess your actions and enable yourself to comprehend your inner light, alter your insights; for example, with an affirmation such as this:

"I am a loving person and I believe in loving people."

When we observe that humanity is despairingly over-wrought by difficulties and challenges, we begin to dissipate within ourselves—for all time—the false belief that humanity's inherent tendencies of unspeakable destruction are truisms of our individual nature. Then we reassess our hopes and dreams and their viability as a depiction of humankind's potential, because whatever we personally experience, humanity will experience eventually. Whatever we personally aspire to as ideal, humanity will aspire to eventually, because each of us is a single cell within the whole.

When you are shaping your new Self, your insights direct the movement of the consciousness of the whole and your considerable individual leverage affects the order of society toward higher sensitivity and awareness. This is so because when you accept yourself as instrumental to reality, you begin reestablishing the universal powers as a shaping force in your life and, with a view of respect, you understand that society is redesigning based upon mutuality in people's points of view.

As we restyle the way we think and behave, we accept that every person is a part of all humanity and is a living consciousness extended both from and to the whole. This vision defines our personal experiences as a member of the social stream. Shifting perception becomes not something that happens to us without our knowledge or awareness, but that results from our individual conceptualizing of what can be and our personal effort toward being more compassionate and amused about the less desirable experiences of this world. We are then better able to manage our emotions and better align our passions.

Humanity is beginning to formulate this kind of world.

The new society is becoming realized fundamentally. All that we perceive as truth is to some degree subject to change, depending upon what we perceive truth to be.

When our mind is open to envisioning that truth is subjective, for the most part, we realize that all of our experiences in life are subjective. This realization expands our ability to comprehend, integrate, allow, enjoy and forgive, because we then have increased our capacity to see others as precious and integral to the whole of life, to realize that every person is necessary because each of us contributes through our own processes.

Through our unique desires, wills, and actions born from self-esteem, we are recreating society. Through our visions, anticipation and certainty, we are reshaping the world. Our individual and joint lives reflect the consciousness of humanity. Integrated as a truth, this is the foundation of the new strategy upon which all of humanity soon will begin to live.

THE PRESENT
AS IT IS COMPLETING

LET US evaluate our lives as they are today. What are we defusing emotionally? What are we reconstructing?

We have been instituted socially to believe in our "voidness," which has made it difficult to discover our higher Nature. Yet as we improve in optimism, humanity is undergoing a change in point of view about what is healthy in our actions toward others.

Everything each of us is now devoting ourselves to—helping others, feeding others, teaching others—is like feeding a garden at the root level. We are watching humanity grow step by step. This is the process of the human race becoming stronger and wiser.

Wisdom is innate in the human spirit. Every person can access higher wisdom. Every person can be alive with the spirit of the Divine. When we align with our personal purpose in life, we know that what we attend to carefully, consistently, and continuously will result eventually in the very fulfillment we seek.

So, how can you believe that all you envision is good for you and you are worthy of it? Instill yourself with those very private contemplations about your own place in the world. Nurture at the root level the seedling of your cosmic being.

Continuous devotion to your vibrant and living spiritual Nature—nurturing a *new* reason for your life to continue—will enable you with hope. Know that your desires and dreams *will* come to pass and that what you know in your inner Self will ring true for others, because our inner experiences, although personal, are simultaneously cosmic.

We are all learning to accept our spiritual power. We are learning that we are connected to The Good and learning to embrace the qualities that constitute a good nature. Every person is essential to the fabric of life. Each person's perceptions are integral to the evolution of humanity into a more fantastic existence than we have ever known.

All that humanity has imagined is now coming to pass. What we have hoped for is birthing. The goodness we have stored and built upon is now taking hold. These centuries have not been a waste of time. The constancy of humanity's common vision is leading us into the realm we have imagined and hoped for.

How can you believe this is so? Listen with your heart. Our hearts guide us clearly and in truth. The *inner knowing self* makes right choices aligned with the Divine for our own benefit and for the benefit of all.

Our individual perspectives and actions are integral to the whole expression unfolding in humanity. When you perceive something enthusiastically within the very essence of your being, there is nothing of which you are incapable, nothing you are unable to do.

The purpose of human life is to learn our own true place in the whole. People want to trust and live in peace. As you reach your zenith of purposeful self-awareness and you feel the summit of your coping skills, you achieve a synchronicity between your physical personality and the delighted Universe.

Our most remarkable achievements are consequences of

the extraordinary contentment that arises from alignment with the inner resonance. When attuned to our higher Nature, we assess our actions in a way that is free of judgment, ridicule, and condemnation. We are no longer perplexed about needing to be perfect. We mature intentionally and with a spiritual reasoning capacity. We understand what will develop our innate kind Nature. We feel our inner spiritual Nature motivating and strengthening us. We resonate in exquisite harmony with all of life.

Humanity can change and grow. It is time to assess our human dramas compassionately. Our ability to comprehend circumstances beyond our current experience is fashioning us into an extraordinary people. All that we have learned to incorporate in our personal awareness is altering the world. As we each come to value our own personality, we can then comprehend our personal strength and contribution to the human drama.

OUR LIVES AS
THEY ARE TRANSCENDING

BY DEVELOPING an honorable temperament, we rise into our admirable true Nature and a life that is amazing and delightfully expanding.

Imagine that humanity has risen from its distemper, that we understand how to be socially successful and we are devoted to being at-one with each other. In the world of tomorrow, we will frequent inner joy more than outer stimulation. We will frequent inspired understanding of various disciplines of self-awareness more than the intoxication of delusions that we will realize are based on fear. We will alleviate our catastrophic pains from excruciating self-judgment by awakening the inner healer. We will devise a respite from the horrible angers that have suffocated our light. We will alleviate the distresses that have suffocated our preciousness. By believing in our oneness, we will alleviate our uncertainty in all of our pursuits.

When we attend to our spiritual Self's grievances, we discover a safe yet healing self-analysis of our most secret fears. We reassess what we care about and what we define as necessary for evolving into our spiritual Nature.

In the times ahead, humanity's behaviors will focus toward self-generating compassion and forgiveness. We will lean on the real distinction between higher actions and ordinary reasoning. We will transcend self-destruction in favor of our wiser Nature. We will believe in the Life Presence as a guiding force for our decisions. We will focus our efforts more humbly. We will no longer be overwhelmed by premises of self-preservation. Rather, we will concentrate on accessing our godselves.

Once humanity has begun integrating this process, we will institute a form of free-thinking that will inspire and uplift us. Self-analysis will be less divisive. We will be more aware of how to enhance our greater Character. We will endow ourselves and each other with hope and belief in esoteric realities. We will no longer restrict our precious Identities to fathomless falsehoods about reality. Rather, we will enjoy unlimited possibilities of perception, which range from "I" to the whole. We will bridge the disenchantment that has been our suffering to believing in honor as the intelligent path, which also is the means by which humanity will survive. We will consider how we are all more alike than different. We will enjoy friendships of many rather than the smothering attachments of a few. We will no longer judge others as false, but will see every person with humor and patience. We will no longer live based upon separation, but will comprehend the singular origin and singular destiny of all humanity.

This change in focus will not take place in a single hour or a single day, but over many decades, many. Nevertheless, the ultimate result of the path humanity is now treading is an assured *group consciousness*. In place of despair, we will nurture confidence. In place of uncertainty, we will nurture fairness. We will lean upon the attributes of being *soul-infused*. This attitude will alter the way we perceive ourselves, until we live instinctually as if no other person is our enemy. We will cooperate, or agonize from the lack of it (until we learn to let go and let be).

As humanity embraces spiritual perceptions, we will embrace our new Identities. We will completely reassess ourselves and believe in our innate extrasensory Nature. We will invoke cosmic awareness as a precious commodity upon which all else depends for our success as a spiritual human being. We will reconsider what is unacceptable behavior, no longer needing to fear being judged or criticized; such actions will be uncommon and we will find them difficult to imagine. We will no longer be overcome by ineptness. Rather, we will know our spiritual power and incorporate it in everything we do. Our lives will then unfold as if by magic. Yet it is natural, because the unfolding is a consequence of healing our attitudes toward ourselves and others. We will so alter our intentions and willfulness that we will no longer fumigate ourselves with ridicule or self-denial. We will comprehend our sensitive spiritual consciousness and be absorbed with developing it.

Humanity, we are a part of each other. Each of us is a single cell within the Cosmic Consciousness we name God. Each of us is a thread within the universal fabric of life. Humanity's survival and existence depends upon us individually grasping the unitary framework of all life forces. Each of us, whom we think of as a separate self, is a reflection of a central *Nature*. Together, we compose a single unit of *Thought Expression*.

In the midst of our strifes and wars, we will begin to see the erroneous and futile misnomers of our previous false perceptions. We will release our concerns over our differences. We will see how each person and living being is an aspect of a whole consciousness. The new society will reflect our innate spiritual Selves. By exploring our unique Character, we will see that we are all alike, merely individually studying facets of this incredible experience we call life.

PART II

How We Can Achieve the New Society:

Individually and As a Whole

BECOMING A NEW HUMAN

OPENING OUR awareness toward hope is the most important thing we can do toward becoming a new human. How is this done?

See yourself gently. Grasp the truth of you, that you are a magnificent spiritual being. Live fully with a conscious mind, tranquil heart, and invigorated physical body. To transcend personality traits that may demoralize you or destroy unity, live consciously with an intention of goodwill, actions of fair-mindedness, and beliefs in honor. To know your bright reflection, totally immerse in your higher awareness. To achieve higher awareness (higher consciousness), alleviate the delusions that may currently define your life. No longer champion hatred or disillusionment; rather, embrace the incredible goodness of your *inner knowing self*. Assume a focus and intention that surpasses disenchantment. Reawaken the inner peace that is limitless, boundless, and continuous. Bridge the differences between you and others.

Forgiveness, tranquillity, and a gentle nature are our innate Character. In those moments when you are free of confusion, you may be enlightened as to the purpose of your life and the purpose of humanity's existence as well as ways to surpass paralyzing fears. Your personal reality depends upon your experiences of various options that come to your awareness. To appreciate your remarkableness, live from the divine perceptions of your *inner knowing self.*

Humanity's true nature and dominant characteristic is a generosity of spirit. When you see this in yourself, that is when you lift into that Identity and live for the good of all. When you actively engage these attributes with all the fervor and blessedness you can muster, that is when you lift into your finest hour and become a light in the world.

You lift into being a new human by living as a representative of all that is good, by reflecting in all of your actions your spiritual Nature, and by giving back to life an abundance of joy in everything you do.

The new humanity begins with each of us aware of our value and actively involved in the experience of being human. Humanity is an extension of our *combined* singleness of mind. The new humanity will be each of us fully realized.

Raising Our Vision of Ourselves

WE ARE all *earthborn*. In the new society, this common perspective will raise our vision of ourselves.

To be unaffected by the conditions in the world and to uplift your vision into higher awareness and reach a calm and balanced spirit:

- Create order in your life.
- Be strong through your inner Character.
- Achieve serendipity by striving to live as a spiritual master every day.
- Explore and use your imagination.
- Keep hope in your plans and promises.
- Enhance yourself through grand disciplines, such as meditation, yoga, prayer.
- Live by new standards: *"Be kind . . . Live humbly."*
- Restore happiness in yourself in every situation.
- Listen carefully to other people's ideas.
- Utilize other people's original thoughts in some way.
- Believe in the essential goodness of every person.
- Live each day fully self-aware and in harmony with all of life.
- Reassess false beliefs that bog down visionary concepts.

- Reach toward life with an open mind toward all people and circumstances.
- Understand that consequences are a reflection of beliefs and attitudes.

Our inner strength is greater than any dilemma. Kindle faith in your capacity to rise above the dilemmas that plague you. Reach out for resourceful solutions; they may seem impossible but the results will be substantial.

Sometimes it does not seem possible to live as our heart wants to. Sometimes it is a great challenge and seems too much to grasp. To uplevel your life:

- Be *still*.
- Live without abrasive interactions.
- Trust that all avenues are accessible when pursued in alignment with a higher cause.
- Believe that your personality is reconstructing and becoming more amenable.
- Believe that all animals have a kindred spirit to humanity.
- Understand that life is an expression of natural spiritual law.
- See every person as a part of a whole force.
- Rearrange your personal agenda if, in the moment, the highest definition of your being requires you to be elsewhere.
- Listen inwardly for the counsel of the angels.
- Reposition your attitudes to surrendering false pride.
- Imagine possibilities.

Saturating our actions and imagination with these criteria stimulates positive change in our lives. Focus on success. And, remember, it is a process.

Historically, humanity has not been cognizant of the values that are now paramount in our culture. It is as if our true Selves have been encased in concrete, as if we have been marble statues, facsimiles of our true Selves. Humanity will become more spiritually aware than we are today. In the times ahead, we will be more introspective, visionary, and intelligent regarding solutions to the difficulties we face. We will better decipher and improvise how to resolve our struggles—because we will be enchanted with our spiritual Nature.

Humanity is approaching a level of living that will surpass known discoveries about styles of communication, complexity, and synchronicity. Human consciousness is stretching in such a way that it will be commonplace to devote ourselves to being reverent toward all. We will engage an extraordinary sense of self-appreciation, which will invoke a capacity to appreciate others. We will believe of others, *"You are glorious."* We will comprehend the range of affections that compose reality and embody those affections in our traits and behaviors. We will feel the presence of the living God in the world around us and no longer be afraid.

Becoming spiritually awake is not remarkable. It is a natural process toward which we are moving. We are being consumed with the fabric of love. Everything we do and say is like a thread of cosmic awareness imprinting itself on our socialization—individually and as a whole.

We are going forward. We are becoming purified of the notions that have burdened our common awareness. We are becoming able to live with a sense of devotion to all that is good. We are becoming one.

HANDLING THE SWIFT
ALTERATIONS IN OUR LIFESTYLES

OUR PURPOSE for being physical is to assess individual values, appreciate the common strengths that guide us, uncover the beauty in our being, and restore an affection for all of life. When we accept our loving Nature, in all situations, we are no longer misguided by desire or greed, because we are at-one with our gentle Self. To maintain equilibrium and energize your spiritual power, expand in awareness and approach higher consciousness as a form of your true identity.

Humanity has forgotten that the whole of us shifts as a result of each person's experiences, that our personality defines our individual process and leads us into avenues previously unknown and untried so that we may grow. When you lift into the higher vision of your *inner knowing self*, you are able to believe in the higher laws that guide you. When you do, you begin living as a natural being.

Walking the path of believing that The Life Forces guide, shelter, protect, and enhance us changes the way we view life. No matter what happens or what dangers possess us, we feel fortunate in our ability to live fairly—with humility and pride, grace and courage, sensitivity and power. These qualities amplify our inner wisdom and direct us so we are able to reach new heights in this world that is ascending in consciousness.

Within a developing embryonic state of being, such as humanity is now experiencing, the effects of a single life force resonate and ripple throughout all other experiences and personalities. Our chief personal responsibility is to live from our spiritual Nature, because living in personality means falling into disarray and chaos by way of emotions and judgments.

You find the inner power by devoting yourself to living to the best of your ability every day. The inner power results from your earnest effort at living in balance with all. The key to maintaining equilibrium during catastrophic occurrences is compassion for yourself and others. The keys to maintaining your spiritual being and spiritual life are compassion and the ability to reason from a higher perspective.

To comprehend catastrophic episodes, look on them from a point of view that is broader than your personal needs and desires:

- Direct and focus your passions to their fullest potential, which extends your mind and presence.
- Live with a true concentration upon the passions that motivate you.
- Acquire concentration as a result of a continuous effort to resonate with all, as if your voice is a single musical note within a great orchestra.
- Reassess continuously what kind of person you are, always improving and attuning to the vision of your inner Nature.
- Bring into your experience this vision of hope and purpose, which are the threads that hold us together in the midst of chaos.

These elements formulate the greatest and deepest mysteries yet enable us to comprehend opportunities that appear.

By living these elements, you live fully in a clear mind rather than be absorbed by confusion or undisciplined reactions.

Your personal destiny is in your own hands; not through effort, but as a function or extension of your concentration. By directing your concentration with all of the splendor you feel moving through you when you pray, you can access the higher intelligence within you. By your greater conviction and closer knitting of the innate spiritual power, you can live as one with the life forces of nature and humanity.

We are living during an era of unparalleled growth of our personalities and spiritual Nature. Whether we are attuned to the world's infatuations or are more interested in being alive with spirit, the world is changing. Patterns of global and personal behaviors are shifting. Everything we are doing is reconstructing us into a frequency of compassion. Within this enormous form of strengthening our spirits, we are grasping attitudes that will shape and fill the world with joy. Some of those attitudes are unfamiliar because we have not relied on our true Nature. Some of the attitudes synchronize with directing our concentration to being more attuned. Everything we conceptualize as necessary becomes a formula for our spiritual being.

As we become more compassionate, we learn that the reality in which we live as an adult is exactly what we have created it to be. When we address our inner consciousness regularly and live within its vibration, we assess our needs and wishes from a different measure. We accept synchronicity as a way of life and differences as potential strengths, and we energize our body through a continuous application of integrity in all that we do. This is what heals us and will heal the world. When you apply a fair portion of effort to your endeavors, you reap an abundance of serendipitous opportunities and circumstances and an abundance of feelings that are sweet and serene.

Potentially, human life is a vision of wonder. The new world we are shaping will extend from our personal beliefs and desires. The new world will reflect the people we are becoming.

What criteria will enable you to live harmoniously?

- Strategize fairly and with equal submission to goodness.
- Visualize harmony in every action and intention.
- Compose formulas of operation that will implement goodwill.
- Surrender self-worship as no longer a model for living.
- Communicate honorably.
- Live with a clear conscience, prepared to modify your behavior patterns if they mislead you.
- Simplify your fraternal obligations.
- Openly attend to all people and beings who cross your way who need service, devotion, or affection.

These guidelines shield us from unnecessary pain and encourage us in directions and to programs for a whole and enhancing lifestyle that is unique and personal. With such behaviors, we are able to rethink any posturing that does not support the whole and able to construct our own posturing to an equitable arrangement with others—because what humanity is about is not rigidity. We are ever evolving, ever reconstructing in our behaviors and visions, ever delineating a more pure expression of the spirit burgeoning from within us.

To make your life sublime, hold a vision of yourself that is lovely, dynamic, and fair. Find a common ground of exchange that enhances your personality.

THE NEW VALUES
AND ETHICAL GUIDELINES

HOW DO your personal judgments, idiosyncrasies, and discriminations influence the populace? What social influences shape your beliefs and values? How can you believe that each person is important and necessary to the well-being of all?

To help create an illumined society, we heal our own negative attitudes and awaken in ourselves new perceptions of what are right actions, right beliefs, and right values. We learn to perceive our innermost Self; how self-will, personal experiences, attitudes, and devotions direct our lives, and that we are integrally connected to every other person.

In the new society, we will be aware of our influences on others in this psychological way just as today we are aware of the effect of the physical environment on our health. In fact, the psychological and physical are synchronous; each affects the other. What we "stew" about mentally sets a tone and energy pattern in the world around us. This expanding vibration, like a stone thrown into a pond, generates pathological reasoning and behaviors that result in antipathy, apathy, judgment, sarcasm, and willfulness, at the expense of everyone. If we expend such an energy, we ourselves are not shielded from the effects; in fact, self is the most affected. More than that, we imbue our personal pattern of self-deception on all humanity—because we are a part of the world and everything any one does influences everyone else.

The human personality requires attunements just as an automobile require tune-ups. Our body and psyche are vehicles of our spiritual consciousness. Following are attitudes that cause us to be less than we are: We credit ourselves with imagination yet dilute our potency by muddying our aspirations by being bitter, critical, or disagreeable; we pollute the social strata with unkept promises and bemoanings of lost dreams; we weaken our spiritual strength and guidance by ridiculing others; we live with conflicting decisions and do not anticipate harmony, rather we succumb to disharmony as natural and we regard failure as natural; we perceive recklessness as exciting and see it as imposing a godlike power; we subjugate insight and intuition as meaningless drivel; we compromise sensitivity, calling it stupidity; and we complain repeatedly and dramatically.

We of humanity are about to straighten out in our lives a composition of vital viewpoints and realizations. We may be unused to serendipity as a way of life, yet such grace truly can be our reality, says *The Mind Within*. We can learn to exhibit a state of mind and emotions that revere life and honor others; because when we feel worthy, we see worth in others.

To attune to your spiritual being and grasp the vital traces of your potent Self, affirm:

"I am an aspect of the Divine Mind and Divine Will, a living expression of the whole of life. Everything I do matters, for me and for others. I live every day instilled with the vital presence of Mind, to be an asset to the world around me. I vitalize my uniqueness and awaken creativity within me, from which comes instinct, insight, intuition, and knowing. I choose, will, and behave in accordance with the laws of the universe and the goodwill of all."

To live as an enlightened person, be thoughtful and conscientious in all avenues of experience. To change the way you exist, choose to live by values that enhance everyone. To acquire trust, be devoted to the higher presence of Mind. Realize that all people suffer because you also have suffered. Explore your personal presence as an example of the Creative Power. Assume a higher framework of action and sensitivity. Applaud your mistakes as ingredients to nurture further trust of the higher powers. If engulfed by errors, turn your attention to higher consciousness, within which you may analyze situations and attain wisdom and guidelines to help you change your circumstances. If things go wrong, turn to the wisdom *within* for direction and to access perceptions that can lead to new directions and opportunities that before you could not imagine.

Historically, we humans fear what we do not understand. A wise person seeks understanding of the unusual and unfamiliar. By investing yourself with the processes of inner linking with the Causative Consciousness, you can realize how valuable you are and how valuable each person is. Even if you feel inconsequential compared to the Universal Presence, when you absorb that Presence into your focus of being, you stretch into realms of thought and belief that previously may have been beyond your capacity to comprehend. This discovery fills you with such hope that you live truly in devotion to your higher reasoning Self. You learn, thereby, to structure your existence based on living the ideals of the spiritual world. When you do, you find that life extraordinarily transforms into a passionate reflection of your greatest dreams.

If you have struggled with the challenges of life, when you walk the pathway of higher sensitivity, you may glimpse, then embrace, a perception something like this:

"Anything I am, I can change today. Anything I have been, I can alter in this moment. What I wish to be, I can be—through my dedication and my thoughts toward that."

Sometimes, it may seem difficult to believe you can release the discordant and inept aspects of your character, that you can dismiss them like an old coat and be new. But you can—by embodying the living force in your daily life in every experience; by not allowing your old character to drive you, to be driven only by your *inner knowing self*'s inspirations in your heart, knowing that what you wish in your spiritual consciousness is your personal truth and *will* come to pass.

We learn to believe. Incorporating belief comes with discipline. We develop compassion, energy, and spiritual reasoning through a program of daily ritual.

Through your continued devotion, day in and day out, to living from your spiritual Self's perceptions, you are better able to reconstruct your foibles and successfully analyze your whole potential existence. When you open your being to frequenting the inner place of harmony, you develop a familiarity with that Energy—until nothing else is real to you except the most necessary belief that you are able to fully express your spiritual Self in your life. Even if you forget how to be in harmony, you are able to recover the procedure with this potent attitude:

"Let me live in harmony with all of life."

Instilling this attitude in every breath, infusing this attitude in every moment, embracing this attitude in every encounter and every action, alters your experiences to feeling totally at-one with life's glorious aspects.

The most significant lesson learned on the inner pathway

is to believe in yourself regardless of disillusionment. When you endeavor to harmonize, you reap the reward of feeling at peace and nothing can discourage you.

Presence is a powerful concept we learn to engage as a force of mind and action. When you decide to live from the strength of your spirit, you open your awareness to a multitude of options, which includes embracing what before threatened or frightened you. You courageously devote yourself to overcoming the qualities and circumstances you may have felt were destructive. You learn to be strong through the energy and awareness of your spiritual Nature, to know that you can overcome the personality weaknesses that have burdened your life. The time comes when you no longer function as you did. The only reality you know is the one blossoming within you and spreading itself out about you—like the new earth—born from your innate sweetness and born from your courage.

Spiritual discipline is the crux of the new society, discipline to vitalizing the whole Self because it takes consistency of action to be a new human. Discipline in habits and in practicing the attunement reaches into the psyche and changes the metabolic structure of the body. Discipline of viewpoints and words alters your experience with others and restructures your personality's secrets, which open, unfold, heal, and dry up—and you recover. When we focus on resynergizing hope in our endeavors, and we hold to that hope with every fiber of our being, what we aim toward and move toward regularly begins to shape into the very reality we have sought.

We are capable of accomplishing our heart-felt goals. Continuity of belief takes us there. By our actions and attitudes, most significantly we create the world we live in. The way we experience life is an expression of our innermost process. How we view the circumstances in which we live—endeavors, relationships, and their tenor—reflect our ability to fully live our potent Character. When we diligently pursue what we know is our best choice, we find it, because our inner being cries to be heard and to be given its fullest expansion of opportunity.

Everything humanity wishes to be is now shaping within us individually. In our inner lives, we are maturing abundantly. We are becoming intuitively discerning and powerfully able to visualize and manifest. In our outer lives, we are practicing making these truths apparent in our reality—until life will become exactly what we have envisioned. It is imperative to hold to your vision and know it is your truth.

To alter humanity's total experience, alter your own experiences. The consequences eventually will manifest for the whole, because what we are, the world is.

OUR NEW ATTITUDE

IN THE basic training of our psyche, we learn to embody the full capacity of our spiritual being. We drink in our divine Nature. We engage the Divine Mind. We blink with the Mind through the consciousness of our soul's presence, which itself is a living force distinct from our personality.

To relinquish your unknowing self and embrace continuously your powerful Identity:

- Open your heart and mind and define life by the Universal Powers that guide you.
- Believe that those Powers illuminate your existence, and realign your focus toward a higher cause and purpose.
- Live the laws of life to the best of your ability every day.
- Stop playing games of self-doubt, self-judgment, and "woe-is-me."
- Responsibly share with others what wisdom you learn.
- Learn to believe in the unseen Presences who give you their counsel and train you in your exquisite capacities as a spiritual being, which you use as a vehicle for your life.

On the path of deepening awareness:

- We release all conditions that have blocked our happiness.
- We forgive every individual who has saddened our experience.
- We participate in activities that lift our sense of well-being.
- We gently applaud our own insights.
- We courageously venture forth in the hope of acquiring serenity.
- We acquire knowledge as a tool of the Divine.
- We listen to the powerful quiet *voice* within us.

Following these criteria leads us to a quiet yet profound perception of our own unique capacity to be whole, majestic, and extraordinarily happy. We heal our soul wounds and learn self-affection, self-love, and courage. We discover the unseen Constituents who are our guiding lights.

All of society is reconstructing. We are renewing our links with each other and with our spiritual Selves. We are rising into a greater synchronicity with the forces of existence, in ways we have yet to ascertain. For the good of all and our own satisfaction, humanity is acquiring a state of being that will encompass holiness.

It is possible to heal the wounds of your psyche. You are capable of behavior modifications that will teach you compassion and bring you into a new form of living. Nothing is more powerful in this world than our minds and the divine beings we are.

Humanity is rising. We will forget the anguish and no longer subject ourselves to dismay and struggle. The day will come when we will have learned a greater focus of existence.

That greater focus is compassion for ourselves and each other. Life will reflect our innate loveliness. We will exemplify the flawless Nature with which we were born.

We did not come into life subject to a God who desires to control or frighten us. We did not come into life with inhibitions. We did not come into life with restraints upon our spirits. We grew these, and we can undo them. We can undo our suffering. The greatest healer—the natural state of our being—is to love one another, in spite of our distinctions; to love one another, in spite of our fears; to love one another with all of the will within us for something better. As we do, we will be raised in our vision and begin to heal our pasts.

OUR NEW HEART

THE ERA we are entering will bring a psychological break-through for humanity. It is a serendipitous moment in the infinite spirit of humankind. This extraordinary experience we are exploring together is consciousness expansion, and consciousness is not mental but is of the heart. Consciousness is that place in the whole Self that is open to surrendering judgment and fear, willing to cooperate and find a middle ground of understanding. Consciousness is the breadth of our whole being, the center of our being, our spiritual Nature. Consciousness is *us* without fear, remorse, anxiety, or judgment.

Until we learn to live in grace and composure, we are surrounded by discomfort and we strive to relinquish the animosity that suffocates us. This becomes a powerful exercise because, while we desire to achieve a higher presence and envision our potential, we are also recovering from many lifetimes of suffering. This latter component has shaped the human personality more than dissension or astrological influences. The essential Personality of our spiritual Nature comprises the criteria by which we evolve.

When we are aggressive, our spiritual Self suffers. When we are generous and resonate with a fresh acceptance of beauty, our spiritual Self is unafraid and realizes a kinship with others. When we are free of disgust, our life is harmonious. The equilibrium of our consciousness depends on the degree of love we invoke from our deep, eternal, and divine Personality.

In the overview of human consciousness, it is quite acceptable to devise strategies by which to unlock our innate inner goodness and embrace the naturally spontaneous spirit we are. When we do, we complement the esoteric side of life from which comes the visionary talents that give direction and create a yearning to live wholly. This formidable situation imposes itself on our behaviors—until we become critically involved with the spiritual frequencies and we simplify our life to a more harmonious existence.

Having an open heart is one of the most necessary characteristics we develop as we rise into the new energy, because until we are able to look upon others with humility and honor their presence, we have learned nothing of any real value for our own growth. When we judge any other, we ourselves are judged. Love is the natural human state. Freely expressing our inclination to forgive and to understand the frailties of human nature does us all much good.

Certainly, sometimes you may have good reason to feel angry or pained over another person's actions. Yet how can you live if all you think about is anger and pain? How can you move forward if you are unable to let go of that bondage that ties us to your past? It is time to let go, accept what is, and resolve to be a better person for it.

Most significantly, we of humanity are learning respect. We are learning that the highest good of all depends on each of us living in harmony. The human race is evolving to its full potential by each of us who is striving to be a better person and is contributing to the betterment of society. By each person who is helping to heal the planet and better influence the children (who are conscious, aware, and present in the light of divine understanding), the human race is acquiring a new awareness and perspective for how to heal the earth and the problems that have plagued us. The human race will survive because we are improving our social patterns and learning to cooperate with people we do not understand.

Compassion is the resolve needed to correct the ills of society. With compassion, we are able to imagine alternatives and we are lifted into the joyous possibilities of a global vision that can seed a world that is balanced and carefree.

The true measure of whether you are accomplishing your goals is your willing application of the principles by which you live in your mind. Living from your heart with a clarity of purpose, understanding, and compassion will improve your life immediately.

OUR NEW PERCEPTION

WHEN IN the spiritual level of perception, we do not get upset, we are not persuaded to be angry, and we do not feel disturbed, because we have learned ways to deal with these emotions. This is humanity's future.

When you use your inner wisdom, you can live tranquilly without feeling shaken by circumstances. You remain *still* in the eye of the storm. You feel calm and at peace and unwilling to lose your position of harmony even if you are in error or inadvertently caused a disturbance. In the flow of the inner reality, you trust that everything will unfold appropriately and without undue distress.

These are the features that will most create the new society. With these qualities in your feelings and behaviors, you are not afraid of what will become of you. You walk through the shadows of the world without flinching. You release and commit to remain in your peaceful state of mind. You decide you are unwilling to be angry. You even forget what it is like to be angry. You measurably learn not to be upset over what previously would have upset you. Even though by rights you may be entitled to be upset, you are not, which makes your life much easier.

When we relinquish control of our lives to a peace-loving focus, we no longer denounce others because we remember that we also err. Others may be frustrated when we are not angry, resistant or reluctant, but we remain calm and clear by our decision and choice to remain so.

Such a state of mind is a primary facility of the spiritual consciousness. The precious beliefs that humanity will cherish in the new society will bid us all toward a calm and clear presence of mind in all circumstances. We will acquire the passion of complementing others. We will fully appreciate our relationships, viewing them as opportunities to temper a kind nature in us. We will see others as expressions of ourselves and realize that each relationship reflects our own evolving Self.

When you perceive others as essential components of your sensitivity training, you see them in a clear and enhanced light, rather than judge them. You accept that you have a personal liaison with them because of what you both can learn during the time shared. This attitude releases the stranglehold of your expectations, and you comprehend that each relationship is a free expression of mutual beliefs and needs.

As we wean ourselves from harmful dependencies, characteristically we decide to let go of controlling the outcomes of our encounters. Uniquely, we prefer relationships that fulfill our need to be aligned spiritually, mentally, and emotionally. When complemented by people who fairly estimate and challenge our attitudes and behaviors, we reason even more astutely.

Ultimately, this will prove to be the most powerful technique to polish humanity's senses as expanding Selves, because relationships hone us in a way that is not otherwise possible. With this clear understanding, we better appreciate our relationships. We evaluate new encounters not for what we desire from them but for the esoteric implications they have toward helping us shape our own true Selves.

In the times ahead, we will be resistant only for as long as we feel angry. We will no longer perceive others falsely, because we will no longer admonish ourselves for our disillusionments and frustrations. If we do inwardly refuse to take charge of our own lives, hoping someone else will lift us out of our misery, it will be because we are afraid of fully expressing our spiritual power—although that is not possible and, no matter how it seems, it cannot be.

You have the power to change your personal point of view regarding self-enhancement, self-appreciation, and self-love. Understanding these qualities is when you alter the course of your life. That is when the path you follow reaches a turning point and you see choices that previously you could not imagine. Then, in a very clearly defined process, you distinctly comprehend who you are. You no longer resist your soul's awareness that is struggling to rise into your waking consciousness. You no longer fear the precious insights that guide, protect, and inspire you. You see that your experiences are a doorway to your whole Self. You realize that every experience strengthens you in some way. Thus, you become more attuned to the spiritual being you are.

Coming to terms with our personal strength and compassion is why we are in life, a reason we are physical, a reason we explore how to be more of the person we feel we can be. It is truly fortunate when you begin to see that life is a fabrication of your soul's needs and not an unavoidable kink around which you must move. Once you take hold of each encounter with an outlook of self-realization, through an exchange of ideas and energy, you heal the discrepancies in your character that have blocked your self-esteem.

In our lives that are filled with interactions and experiences of a physical nature, sometimes we overlook the importance of the spiritual Self's viewpoint. However, once we evaluate each moment as an opportunity, we become more attuned to the synchronicities of life and open-minded to what might develop.

Let us comprehend the inner voice's relationship to the conditions in the world. The inner counselor is more precious in our whole experience than living in the framework called "instinctive." Being able to advise ourselves from the inner wisdom is supra-intelligent, supra-instinctual, and is beyond personal experience; it surpasses any logical alternative.

Inner reality perceptions can heal personal social dysfunctions effectively; in fact, can clarify your emotions and strengthen your sensitivities so you are less gullible and more aware. Consequently, when you envision yourself in comparatively friendly circumstances with people you trust, not only are you able to perceive through the usual senses but you are able to invoke a clarity of understanding that amplifies all possible premises upon which to base decisions.

For a joyful and sane life and personal survival, it is critical to connect with the *inner knowing self*'s clear counsel. By aligning with that point of view, in your life and relationships, you learn to attract blessings rather than distresses. You value yourself as inherently spiritual. To others, you communicate as a person vested with sensitivity, compassion, and enlightenment. You realize it is your inner Self who is living the physical life; your inner Self who is experiencing the world, learning from the world, and giving to the world; your inner Self who is the student of life and your teacher.

To align with your most viable Character and tap the core of your being—your essential Self—focus on creating harmony and alleviating dissonance. Focus on healing misunderstandings and invoking the perceptions of your kinder, attuned Self.

FINDING OUR TOLERANCE

OUR INNER SELF fashions our choices and decisions from a higher perspective about how we may best develop the qualities of our true Character. This is best defined as conscience in control. The true conscience is the voice of the spiritual Self, not the subconscious recordings of the childhood. When we are attuned to being useful to others and grateful for each day we exist, our conscience is the voice of God. A clear conscience is the still soft inner voice that guides us with love and patience. However, when we are not aligned with the qualities of our true being, we are more absorbed in our daily dramas and how to fix the problems we feel overwhelm our lives.

Much more pleasant, and no more difficult, is focusing on our inner being as the model of character we can and must be and to live that Character consciously every day to the best of our ability. When we purposely seek the freedom that comes from a clear mind and clear heart, our attitude is to give-give-give of our truth, our clarity, and our assessment as a spiritually-centered person. Such an attitude restores self-esteem and heals the feeling of being separate from others. With such an attitude, we realize that we need others to feel connected to life. Without that connection, we may feel as if we are floundering without a purpose, goal, or reason for being, which is the focal point that directs our actions in life.

When open to living based on kindness and goodwill, we can forgive ourselves and others. This attitude is an essential functioning trait for our psyche, after which a willingness to explore other ways of being blessed evolves in our mental development. For example, can you forgive yourself and others for tragedies wrought in an unconscious state?

We are each responsible for our own actions, and we each know what amends we must make. That is a part of spiritual learning, of becoming strong and reasoning toward living more usefully.

To forgive yourself, live the new attitudes to the best of your ability. Focus not on anger or anguish. Focus on healing your fears and conditioned reflexes.

How can you forgive others for their despicable beliefs and judgments against you? How can you forgive people for their reflexes that have caused you pain or suffering? How can you forgive people whose great venomous behaviors have changed your life?

In your heart—for *your* peace.

When aligned, we are free of judgment. We see that every person has the inner counselor available. We see their struggle to acquire balance, yet their inability to imagine or comprehend their spiritual power; consequently, they reach beyond themselves with a destructive vibration.

When another person causes you harm—physical or psychological—distinguish between that person's actions/ behaviors/attitudes from the *soul self* beneath that is struggling to survive. Strive to understand that person's pain while, at the same time, act responsibly toward his/her irresponsible actions. For example, in the same way we might take a child who has misbehaved, reprimand that child, and set a condition for recompense without ourselves feeling angry, so we can do with people who have separated themselves from the group consciousness and from their own divine Nature.

In this world of many peoples, while individual identity is valued and worthy, none of us would exist if others were not in the world with us. The primary purpose of aligning to our spiritual being is to recognize that every person is linked with all others, regardless of demeanors, beliefs, appearances, or judgments. On the inner level, every person is a part of a group consciousness that moves as one in the *Void* and breathes as one being. The inner Self focuses attention on lifestyles. The inner Self has a presence of mind that enhances life for the whole.

People who do not live this way do not yet perceive their true Nature or Character and do not fathom their link with others. They separate themselves from the whole by their lack of attunement to the goodness that is within them.

The inner voice is unequivocally the power of the world, the source of wisdom, and the inner teacher for actions that bring joy, heal pain, and free us from ambivalence and uncertainty. Every person on Earth has the inner voice, whether or not they heed it. People who acknowledge this divine voice live a life of concerted effort to being useful, kind, and compassionate. People who deny or ignore the voice are separating themselves from the Divine. As long as they refuse to heed the innate kindness of their souls, they become even more disconnected. Pity them, help them, forgive them. This does not mean allow or tolerate any wrongdoing. It means take firm action but without bludgeoning them with a cruel heart. They do not yet appreciate their responsibility to the whole.

Our task only is to uphold the whole of goodness. The point of view is to respect, appreciate, and honor others.

FINDING OUR VIRTUE

WE WANT peaceful relationships. We want our lives to flow happily and freely. Yet such a life seems uncommon. What can you do to kindle the flame of hope in your life?

- Inspire yourself with the concept that you are capable of resolving differences and negotiating harmony.
- Strive to understand why those people feel differently, why your attitudes and viewpoints are at odds, and accept that.
- Reach a peace *for* others, even if only in your own heart.
- Ascertain your own values and primary needs.
- Reconstruct your own patterns of behavior in your relationships and your place in society.
- Reassess who *you* are, why *you* live, and what *you* can do to help others.

We are unlimited in our capacity to heal the scars of our psyches. In the times ahead, humanity will be fond of sanctity and virtue, which mirror our essential good Selves. Foremost, we will appreciate consideration of people's feelings and needs. By living these attitudes, we will step into a new co-existence. We will see others as our equals. We will overcome our enemy (which is ourselves).

What the world is we are, and what we are the world becomes. Everything we admire about life and social interaction begins *within* as a model of behavior and speech.

To know the purpose of your existence and to know great satisfaction:

- Connect with your spiritual awareness.
- Fuel your imagination.
- Go forward with a new vision of your abilities and new hope for your future.

For strength of character:

- Coalesce your innermost needs into a single concentration: to support yourself and others with compassion, insight, and a serendipitous inclination. As you do, you will begin to plant new possibilities that will build the new society.
- Simplify your interactions into a comprehensive, lovely strategy for resolving differences, anguished cries, and painful memories.
- Live for harmony, and anticipate that harmony is possible. Expect harmony and it will be your truth. Engage this vision daily.
- Comprehend the meaning of your existence by fraternizing with the higher realms of life.
- Heighten your dreams.
- Enhance your capacity to understand.
- Open your heart.

We humans are compassionate beings. When we open our minds to the possibility that we are capable of living from our spiritual Nature, that becomes our truth. Society is not peaceful today, but we can engineer that result—by resuming *stature* as the model for our beings and *quiescence* as the model for our lives. We can turn society around by learning to transcend our fears and worries and to change our viewpoints to living from our innate sweetness.

THE SPIRITUAL LIFE

WHEN LIFE experiences become extremely stressful, we investigate finer reasons for being. We conclude, after searching, that life is more than physical. The following principles best characterize a spiritual life:

- Astute perceptions about all aspects of experience
- An inclination toward matters of the inner Self
- A forgiving Nature
- A living example of kindness
- A generous character.

By living these segments of our true Personality, we are better able to visualize our strength and to embody the qualities in our everyday character. When our main concern is how to be a person of such repute, we begin the arduous task of self-clarifying what we perceive to be necessary for living our truth. We reach a point of no longer feeling the hand of sadness on our brow. Rather, we feel renewed daily through the spirit of the inner kingdom and embraced daily by the spirit of the Universal Mind, or God.

If you are inclined toward the lifestyle of living from your Presence and friendship with the Light, and you fully embody the life principles you have learned to value, what will be the outcome in your behaviors? What will be the consequences of your pursuit toward this way of life? How will you make choices and decisions?

- Live with an aspiration toward fair-mindedness and responsibility for your life. Strive to be an example of the highest resolute being imaginable. We humans are happier when we know we are living according to the universal truth in us, regardless of how circumstances appear to be.
- Value other people's opinions as insightful and practical, as measures that guide your own vision toward the fundamental principles of action for a fulfilling life.
- Sympathize with, acknowledge, and incorporate the shadow side of life—not to allow it to enforce its viewpoint, but to control it (rather than deny it) by your choice of spiritual consciousness in action.
- Breathe in the *cosmic fire,* the prana that saturates all living things. Breathe it in as the very sustenance of your eternal mind and spirit. Breathe it in as the essential fabric of your wholeness, that tangible yet ephemeral substance that links you to all things and all matter.
- Become an admirer of the higher sensitivities that alleviate distresses and irrational inhibitions.
- Open to the power of the universe in your heart and mind and willfully engage in intelligent and insightful occupational pursuits.
- Value and hold in high esteem the opportunities that abound around you for following the path of higher will.
- Join with all spiritual persons who endeavor to awaken the light within, those who are sincere and devoted to all that is good.

- Favor the ability to envision beauty and to comply, with all speed, with those visionary trustees who plant beauty in the world; add your own vision to the whole and live your own life in that regard.
- Achieve synchronicity and compliance with the Divine Presence in your interactions every day.

Our happiest moments are in our agreements with others, wherein bliss infuses us, tranquillity fills us, and we are at peace. When you embody the living principles of the Divine, which you feel and know in the center of your being, you measure the choices of your life by them. For example, you choose:

- Synchronicity as your lifestyle, those seeming miraculous and apparent coincidental events that are natural occurrences in life and are recognized by remaining mentally alert and openly aware of the larger picture of the tapestry of life that connects us all.
- To be fully aware as a higher thinking Self, aware of your innate ability to comprehend the abstract processes of living.
- To actualize solutions to problems through inner wisdom and the guiding instincts of your *inner knowing self.*
- Responsibility, because its value is a form of self-discipline toward self-reliance and self-approval.
- To abide by what represents value to all persons and all living beings, because every person is a member of the human species and a member of the Consciousness manifested.
- To act each day as your spirit wills you and guides you, because the inner Self is the living body of God.
- To achieve wondrous things and to strive toward

wondrous accomplishments, because that is the drive of the Omnipotent within—to stretch itself to be more than it has been.

- To admire and reach through your heart toward all that you know is your innate ability to be.
- To expand in every way possible that your heart inspires you.
- To lift up your beliefs into the realm of knowing that what your heart moves you to pursue is more than a foolish dream and more than for self alone; indeed, it is essential to the very existence of life and to the evolution of all that is holy. (Know that your personal presence and inspiration are a part of that vast movement of the consciousness of the whole and that your own energy and light are needed to keep that *force* active and vital as you ascend into a new identity and individual form of thought and being.)
- To accept that your devotion to your inner promptings and inner guide is worthy and necessary, because it is the Spirit of Life prodding you into realms uncertain and untapped, urging you to explore, investigate and give all that you are, regardless of how unusual you may believe your talents are. Accept this because it is your destiny and your gift to the world.
- To trust that the Universe guides you fairly and that—when you devote your heart and whole being to consciously living the natural laws and applying yourself in every way to acting out the principles that guide you—your efforts will bear fruit.

These are the steps to the precious potency and to embracing God. We make these choices as we step toward a life of inner tranquillity. When you live consciously, with the *voice* of life as your conscience, you are unafraid. You believe in the power that invests you with a vision to understand and apply masterfully all that you feel guided to contribute to the lives and consciousness of others. You value the visions that move through you. You value the wisdom innate in every soul. You know that every person carries the Divine Presence within and that your own viewpoint is no more and no less remarkable.

Everything we are is a part of the greater good of life. Everything we are is an extension of the whole of life. When you daily invest your whole Self—body, mind, and spirit—with whatever techniques, processes, or rituals enable you to tap the center of your being, you reinstill your spiritual alignment. You reach out to others. You take the hands that guide you, teach you, and hold you. All around us are teachers and friends willing to be there for us when we open our hearts to them.

The following components help us invoke spiritual splendor as a daily "food." These qualities are invaluable for visualizing your potential and clarifying your inner strength:

- *Perfectly blending with others.* When you realize that the presence of others affects you, you visualize a greater strength within yourself.
- *Living with curiosity and enjoyment—like a child.* This clarifies your sensitivity to your purpose in life.
- *Appreciating all that comes to you.* When attuned to the serendipitous occurrences in life, simultaneously you become free through the auspicious powers inherent in your being.

The following characteristics represent your presence when you are aligned with your divine purpose:

- You counsel yourself and others with a vision of wholeness and a capacity to bridge the vast range of talents that are innate in your whole Self.
- You visually resonate to living a higher consciousness lifestyle, which daily reinforces that you live sensitively to the magnificent opportunities that abound around you.
- You alleviate your discomfort and kindle your hope by learning to be self-empowered.
- You dedicate to yourself and others—in all that you do—the unique gifts of spirit with which you are blessed.

These characteristics are the essential diet of a successful spiritual life. When you live each day for the highest good of all, you are filled with light.

OUR NEW MIND

PART OF becoming a new human is in evolving mentally. We develop the newer visionary style by awakening our spiritual consciousness and our precious self-esteem. This is the primary need facing humanity today, because until we closely analyze and strengthen our connection with our *inner knowing self,* we are nothing more than a body aware of being human. However, once we identify that we are a spirit in a body, we coordinate the activities of our life to be spiritual as well as physical. Everything we express as a physical being becomes extraordinarily simple; because once we analyze our nature as an evolving spiritual being, we are no longer unsure of who we are. We define our precious life as an opportunity to learn more about our spirit, which aligns us and clears our thoughts. Our life then becomes truly successful, with quality and meaning in our innermost sacred accomplishments. Even recognition does not affect our decisions. When aligned mentally and devoted to the principles of life that guide us, nothing of this world can sway us. Our thoughts are shaped by our beliefs in higher thought.

You awaken the *delight* through understanding the significance of being mentally attuned to the Divine which guides you in everyday activities. When filled with a clear appreciation of the inner counselor, your day-to-day actions become harmonious and without anticipation or anxiety. Rather, you live to be appreciated only for your sanctified actions. All else becomes irrelevant.

When imbued with the spiritual frequencies of thought and intuition, we are sedate in our manner and speech. We do not appeal for recognition or seek appreciation. We are not anxious about whether we will be understood, not confused about the various feelings that define conscious living, not unsure of our actions. With a sense of blessing, we calmly decide to activate the natural thinking processes that are a blend of the Universal Mind with our own innermost sacred Self.

In strategizing the potential union with our spiritual Self, we attain precise visions and interpretations of cosmic delight. We feel at-one and begin to live this practically with others. Using this criterion, we evaluate our own processes when we are not at-one with the Universal Mind; because when synergizing the thinking process with our inner counselor's vision, we are advancing as a soul in a physical body.

Being human has a range of possibilities. First, we attain the clear vision toward which we have aspired for many eons, we recognize the state of mind called God, and we are attracted to the spiritual being we will become. Once open to this system of interpretation, our clarity and distinctive focus come into play and hope enforces within us inner promptings to live from our light.

OUR NEW BODY

THE NEW REALITY is taking over one person at a time in our changing perceptions and attitudes. The new world will take over individually long before everyone on Earth will transform. That is why it is important to identify how we evolve into the lighter frequency physical body.

Who you are constitutes not only your personal thoughts but also your physical form. The human body frequently refines, changing shape, density, appearance, and health. Scientists say that the cells of the body actually completely change every seven years. Beyond the effect of basic genetic makeup and mental habits, at this time in human history, according to *The Mind Within*, the human body is in transition to its next evolutionary stage.

Material existence operates on different levels of frequency. Some frequencies, or degrees of vibration, are more dense, such as ice; others may be less dense, such as water, vapor, or air. In a similar way, the physical body is changing its level of vibratory frequency to a more refined degree.

There are some significant differences between the current third dimension physical body (the one most humans have now) and the new higher vibrational physical body (that results from living the new awareness). Both forms decay, but the newer body decays more slowly; for a longer period of time, the higher frequency body resists destroying vibrations (disease) that cause disintegration.

Over time, it will become obvious to humanity that the body's disintegration results from personality dysfunction(s), self-disillusionment, and/or a fascination for destroying habits and attitudes; essentially, physical disintegration results from foolish behaviors and choices.

The Mind Within says that our most foolish belief—and perhaps the most destructive effect on our health—is accepting that we cannot reach and live from the sensitivity of our spiritual consciousness. *The Mind Within* also describes foolishness as believing that (1) we function independently of others, (2) cannot show responsibility without becoming absorbed by others' demands, (3) must be controlling to avoid losing ourselves, and (4) regard ourselves as failures. *The Mind Within* says we only fail when we no longer try.

Humanity's higher purpose is to invoke spiritual consciousness by how we take care of our bodies. Alignment with the inner Self invokes wellness. In the new human body, ideally we consume higher force foods that uplift us physically as well as mentally (e.g., *live* foods such as blue-green algae, sprouts, vegetables and fruits that have not been depleted of their natural abundance of vitamins, minerals, and enzymes). The reason is that biologically our body is an energy field and the foods we eat are energy; when we consume foods that are impure, we are depleting the energy source that keeps the body functioning efficiently. Because the body is organic, it needs proper fuel in much the same way that machines need proper care (e.g., cars, computers). Improper fuel "gums up" the body's operation, clogs the "pipelines," and corrodes the tissues.

In the times ahead, humanity will desire to function mentally at an optimum potential and we will realize that certain foods affect our ability to think clearly. To acquire a more clear consciousness, one of the first elements to discern is what to eat for your individual body and chemistry. Observe how your body feels and reacts to particular foods. If a food causes you to feel disgruntled or to dislike yourself, it is a negative effect beginning to destroy your brain cells; disease continues from there. To feel completely aligned with your spiritual power and not overwhelmed by the forces of life, eat for consciousness.

What foods are beneficial and what foods are harmful to your body? When you feel flushed with an increased level of energy, the food you are eating is giving you strength. When you feel a creative burst of awareness while eating and are stimulated mentally, you are eating a food of higher causative force. When you feel energized by what you eat and move quickly through the meal, to get on with your focus of the day, that food is a productive vibrational stimulation. Any time you are consciously aware of synthesis mentally and emotionally and your body feels invigorated, that food is supporting your spiritual consciousness.

The other side is foods that dampen the spirit. While eating, if you feel tired, sleepy, disgruntled, uncomfortable, confused, or dysfunctional, that food is unclear or unproductive for maintaining a higher energy field and ideal physical body. Such a food may not affect someone else negatively, but due to your unique chemistry or sensitivity that food may have such an effect on you. This applies to any food that causes a disagreeable reaction in your body, emotions, or mental clarity. Foods that cause you to feel out of sorts, unsettled, angry, impatient, or frustrated, are foods that stimulate the lower energy field. Any symptoms that are immediate or within an hour after eating—such as disorientation, loss of power, dismay, or discouragement—indicate you have eaten something that lowers your concentration and, thereby, deters your energy level; any symptoms such as feeling disturbed or ambivalent complicate the state of wellness. *The Mind Within* recommends that you completely avoid such a food.

If you strangle, gag or choke while eating, or soon after, your body is rejecting a food and it is wise to discontinue eating it altogether. Any sensation in your body, in any part of the body, while eating or within the first hour after eating, indicates a food allergy that is uncomfortable at least, and may be destructive. What may begin as a mild reaction, if the food is ingested regularly can become quite serious; such a food is best avoided for an extended time—such as one year—to allow the body to heal and gain new strength before experimenting with that food again. In some cases, the food may be reabsorbed, or you may never be able to tolerate it.

Consuming lower vibrational foods does not nurture our spiritual power. We are advised by *The Mind Within* to choose foods that are filled with the force of life, such as fresh herbs from a garden and vegetables that have not been overcooked or tainted by toxins. Also recommended is fewer, minimal, or no meats. Such a program gives us the ability to think clearly, feel physically powerful and vitalized, and emotionally in harmony and at peace. These are general answers, yet provide a comfortable lifestyle.

Sometimes, we humans abuse the body. When this affects our happiness, it is devastating and even critical to the life span. It is significantly even more so with the new higher vibrational body, because not only is that body overwhelmed physically but at the very least we also lose the ability to perceive from higher awareness, and we may lose clear comprehension of our life purpose and life direction.

It is very precious when you realize that you need a well physical body in order to activate most effectively the new level of vibration on Earth. When your body is not functioning in its purest state possible, you are not able to tolerate the energy shifts without feeling the "uplifting" as a force preventing you from evolving. Your actions and attitudes in the new direction then feel like weights holding you back.

Interestingly, when we assume a personality shift (by centering on the divine inner knowing) causatively we also affect others. So, how you view yourself and the world closely attunes with the principles you learn to appreciate in your newer vision of prosperous thinking and living. It is essential, therefore, to visualize yourself as whole and to live accordingly—by your inner knowing characteristics that elevate your desires, yearnings, and the capacity to eat well and live harmoniously.

To live wholly, with peace of mind and delight:

- Realize that every encounter serves as a form of motivation toward your goals.
- Surrender your needs to your *inner knowing self*'s inherent characteristics and desires.
- Live in humility, to show that you value others.
- Comprehend your place in life.
- Reach out for understanding.
- Understand that you causatively affect the world around you by your choices and actions.
- Formulate a plan of action that reflects your divine being and purpose.
- Visualize your capacity to be more tolerant.
- Concertedly apply your whole experience of the moment toward fully endowing others through your generosity of spirit and being.
- Value every moment of your life.
- Utilize all of your experiences as a "voice" for your future needs.

By allowing your spiritual Self to fill you, you are more confident and you absorb the necessary listening qualities to be aware of the universal powers that impact us every day. To go forward with a new consciousness and reasoning power, forgive your blunders and allow your *inner knowing self*'s values to clear the way for what you do in life. To illuminate your new being and body, live in your powerful Presence at all times and express that focus through your decisions and actions. To bear fruit, live your whole truth, lift yourself into your highest capacity of forgiveness, and listen to the guiding force in your heart for why you were born. To embrace your new and more complete Self, attend to your physical being.

FINDING OUR COMPASSION

THE MIND WITHIN says that earthquakes, floods, and tidal waves will increase during the 21st century. If that is true, how do we acquire and exude tranquillity?

Compassion heals a worrying nature—a compassion for all of our struggles. As we grow in the capacity to be affectionate and loving toward all, we learn compassion, which is the depth of our spirit.

To acquire compassion:

- Linger daily in your spiritual Identity.
- Spend time courting your spiritual Persona—until it takes over in your attitudes and actions.
- Live by the principles of powerful inner direction, which will motivate you to be compassionate and able to heal all of your strife.
- Listen from your *inner knowing self.*
- Adhere to your inner counselor's advice.
- Determine that you are "musically" sensitized to all vibrations and sounds; acquire higher senses to engage the tones of majestic expression.
- Engage the Supreme Mind's energy force as your own dear wisdom, through which you surround yourself with a force-field of protection against all catastrophic conditions, events, and circumstances.

- Free your expectations and do not compromise with any person regarding the advice of your *inner knowing self*. Listen only to your inner counselor when faced with ridicule or objection. Devote yourself to your inner counselor's wise direction for your existence.

- If you sometimes admonish yourself or others for indiscretions, this is of little importance overall. Of greater value—for acquiring the inner power—is to subject yourself truthfully to the ways of harmony you see before you. Any practice or endeavor that is not in harmony with your own experience, do not engage in, pursue, or allow in your contemplations.

- Awaken sensitivity to your spiritual Identity, through which you will seed conceptual perceptions and a lack of bias and judgment. This will clear a path through your psyche—beyond distresses and fears—into the clear space of your inner being. You will discover your capacity for forgiveness, hope and understanding, and you will be willing to leave behind what has burdened you. You will no longer be overcome by all you have struggled with. You will no longer judge your present by your past. You will no longer be afraid to surrender to the power of the Universal Light that you sense guides you.

- Although frequently you may still be perplexed, begin to drop behaviors that are not your true Self. Exist solely within the protection of a kind demeanor and a sincere devotion to being thoughtful, courageous, and forthright. Flow with appropriate actions effortlessly and without preconception. Concentrate and focus through your *inner knowing self*.

- Believe in your potential extraordinary capacity for being wholly at-one with your quiescent Self and devoted to what we identify as God.

- Find life amusing, with an attitude of delight and childlike whimsy that flows through you like a gentle summer breeze, passing beyond you like the fragrance of summer lilies, gently surrounding and caressing all of life that you touch by your presence.

- Become amazed at the wonders of life, at the intricacies of the power, and at the brilliant fascinations you have had for acquiring intellectual pursuits. Become amazed at the quandaries you have allowed yourself to fall into by a lack of insight. Become amazed at the capacity you have had for anguish. Learn that, indeed, you can be *still* in the midst of all around you. You can be *quiet* in the midst of fear and confusion. You can be so aligned that you are truly devoted to the inner power that guides you. In this way, serendipitously you encounter life, embrace every person, and joyously expect that all you do and all you hope for will indeed be fortuitous for everyone. You no longer hope only for your own sanctity, but you hope for the sanctity of all living forms. You breathe serenity as your power increases, and you devote yourself to fully integrating a joyous state of being.

- At this point, you begin to tap the core of your being, thereby realizing your capacity for being compassionate toward all persons and circumstances.

When you live compassionately, you are not devoured by necessity or desire. You walk in the midst of despair and it touches you not. You live from an attitude of oneness with the Cosmic Consciousness that guides you. In your complete Stature, you are at peace.

THE DOORWAY

ACCESS THE center of your being by letting go of limiting what you believe is true. By releasing judgment, you open your heart to the inner voice, which offers understanding. The inner voice is the inner counselor/inner teacher that guides us on how to live well.

When we deny the counsel of the still, small inner voice, we lose ourselves, because without that counsel we wander aimlessly and have no grasp of how to be truly at peace. Sometimes we are unable to perceive the inner voice because it speaks so softly. Sometimes we regress in our ability to live humanely, because it is our spiritual Nature that opens our viewpoint toward living in goodwill and fair-mindedness. To fill your life with serenity, relax your guard against the unfolding of your softness. By relaxing your expectations, you become more gentle and thoughtful and risk more to be happy.

Life is an opportunity to explore how to choose wisely, to evaluate our actions and reconstruct our attitudes. When social demands become less tolerable, increasingly we find ourselves in conflict. At first, we extricate ourselves very slowly from the standards of visionless tyrants who seek to command us mentally and emotionally. Once we learn to walk away from delusions of grandeur and to seek the inner Presence, we find peace of mind. Once we integrate that Presence, we see with uncompromising insight.

By integrating, or fusing, your spiritual consciousness to your personality, you develop the ability to discern between right thought/right action and the mistaken powers of socially-acceptable justice. As you exemplify this, you become truly effective, and only then. Judgments that once caused you grief dissolve. You even forget how to condemn others.

When we are full of the heavenly forces of life, nothing else but that guides our actions. Inherently we observe the atrocities of this world with a centered knowing of their causes. This perception helps us eliminate our own misguided behaviors and to comprehend the greater concepts of life. We even begin to like being human. Being human is a limitation only when you forget that foremost you are a spiritual being. Being human is dangerous only when you have no sense of our whole being. Once you realize that your mind is your "heart" and your mind is your spirit, you train yourself to utilize the full potential of your mind, which is cosmic. The mind is the vehicle through which we are given inspiration, vision, and insight. The mind awakens the inner voice.

Initially, you feed your mind by stretching your capacity to imagine. Through imagination, you tap the Cosmic Consciousness and lean upward toward your true Self, which is boundless. Mind is the expression of the true Self. Mind is the inner doorway to the higher realities and soul.

When you train your mind to observe and listen to your inner senses and inner voice, you are invoking the Universal Thought Stream into your awareness, which then fills you with ideas that stretch your concepts of what is truth. You become able to envision a broader reality than you previously knew or understood. Through the discipline of a clear mind, you touch the universal force called God. Through a disciplined and tutored mind, you hear the clear voice of God, which is soft and gentle.

The voice of the Divine is in everyone. When you train your mind to be *still,* you become able to perceive the small soft voice within you. With a still mind, you can connect with the Divine Presence in a very substantial way. Understanding comes when you are *still.*

To open your spiritual consciousness, concentrate on healing your mind. Heal your mind with prayer, meditation, the study of various spiritual teachings—and laughter!

PART III

Our Heritage and Our Destiny

HUMANITY'S ANCIENT LINKS

THE MIND WITHIN says that in the beginning of life on Earth, humanity already had existed elsewhere for many thousands of years. Humanity did not originate on Earth. Our species began many many eons ago, in another galaxy and on several other planets. We are not the only species in the universe, either. There are several varieties. Humanoid is predominant, but not at all singular in design.

Humanity originated in a universal layer called "etheric density." This was not the third dimension as we know it today, but at the time was the foremost example of how to manifest in a third dimension reality. For many, many eons in the original focus of being, humanoids were unable to procreate. They were not yet male and female, but were the first of their kind and devoted to their own existence. They came into being as a result of the development of materiality by a higher level of existence, which we today know as angels.

When exploring the original philosophies and inner wisdoms, we discover that the angels are more than we have imagined them to be. We learn they are a species of the Universal Consciousness, which, prior to the initial lifetimes in etheric matter, were not physical beings and held only light force and light energy, which is the angels' natural form.

This premise of existence is the original theory of how humans came to be. In order to explore other elementary points of view in reality, some of the angels chose to materialize into a denser body of consciousness, which was multidimensional even then but had not yet been populated by higher intelligences. This chapter identifies humanity's beginnings and how and why each of us is connected—at the very center of our being—to all other forms of life, because without the consciousness of life itself we would not be. Humanity is not central to existence, but is a fraction of it. There are many beings in many realities who carry the signature of the Divine Consciousness.

With evolutionary perceptions of reality, let us realize that the human species is one of many of its kind; humanoid meaning upright, intelligent, and filled with the breath of wisdom. Perhaps this information will become more valuable in humanity's self-estimation once we characterize ourselves as vehicles through which our higher evolved souls came into a third dimension existence in order to purify their frequency vibrations of mind and spirit. Of course, this became necessary only after humanity began. Prior to that time, there were no mistakes in consciousness to warrant such a vehicle. However, since that time, one of the ways we humans evolve is through continuing realities in several lifetimes, both consecutively and in parallel.

When human lives began, we sought the fulfillment of spirituality. This became an obsession—until we forgot who we truly were and lost our inner connection to the total Presence. We obsessed over what we desired and forgot we were already spiritual beings, although incarnate. This minor misunderstanding of what physical life was for led us down a path of ambivalence, misconception, and resistance to our inner knowing, which requires concentration and self-discipline. Therefore, we sought to acquire higher understanding.

Perhaps now humanity can realize that our greatest adventure lies in the inner realities, the dimensions that are within us. The inner worlds are far more fascinating in our perceptions of what is conducive to thought than the many outer worlds we see with our physical vision. In the inner worlds, we discover our power and compassion and, complemently, the voice of All That Is.

Following is the nature of the human species, as we align with other forms of life:

- We are capable of huge mistakes, yet just as capable of discovering incredible alternatives to any circumstance that arises.
- We are just as valid to each other as we are to the Higher Realms who postulate that we were once angels.
- We are able to impress upon our minds visionary strategies that illuminate our worthiness and compatibility. Once we reach the height of our sensory explosions and find the Void within us, we begin to comprehend the eternal spectrum of the All.
- We can become divine as a human being; when we are at our most clear, we are as near to divinity as the angels.
- In all of our voices are the sounds of the universe in its wide ranges of musical tones of which our perceptions are but aspects. In the same way that rainbows reflect the various hues of reality, so our various tones reflect the spectrum of existence in vibration.
- Circumstances align our hopes and develop wisdom in us so we become honorable in our relationships to living in a world that is populated by millions of varieties of the Force, which we call the Divine Mind.
- Essentially, each one of us is a reflection of the most

perfect Presence, which we name God.

- Living in a human form gives us an opportunity to appreciate the finer realities, within which all of the most cherished beings exist, including humans but not limited to humans.

- Suppose we created a species? How would we realize ourselves in it? Is it not perhaps the most extraordinary consideration to acknowledge that human beings are only one example of thousands of conscious life forms that have manifested to fulfill the integral aspects of the whole of life, or consciousness itself?

- Perhaps our humanoid form is but a capsule of the Life Presence so that it may experience itself in the subtler realities.

- Everything we of humanity have been able to conceptualize is but a droplet in the vast ocean of wisdom and experience. Our lives are unlimited, because that of which we are a part is without boundary. Our lives represent the finest forms, which are, by definition, physical yet etheric.

We are not as individual as we seem. We are all bonded by an invisible web of the Life Presence. We are bound by that Presence, which, like an ocean, holds us as one breath and one body. Our individual uniqueness is no more unique than a single perception is unique among all of our thoughts on any given day. We are so intricately connected to all living forms that each one of us is no more distinct in his or her originality than a single cactus is distinct from all other cacti in the desert. We may appear divided. We may even think we are beyond devotion to others. Yet if we do not give our honor and humor in every action, attitude and manner, we are cutting the thread to our own existence, severing the link to our own support to that very existential quality of the Life Force that gives us meaning and the ability that we perceive is independent thought.

We are so integrally bound to all life forms that even our blood is a part of that same ocean of energy. Our individual shapes, colors, and sizes are like the various cells of a single organism. Our individuality helps us convey most effectively our personal evolution of ideas and experiences. Yet, predominantly, all of us are able to visualize and telepathically communicate because of the symmetry of the life force in and through us.

The beginning of wisdom is the realization that there is no true individuality. Individuality is a fashionable interpretation of a Being we do not yet fully understand, a Being we all are compositely—the one we eternally identify as God.

The Mind Within says that frequently we are re-evaluated by our Elders in the cosmic spectrum of the life forces. The human race, as a whole, is redefined genetically on occasion by the Peoples who originally seeded us here. This includes all various creative differences among us, because, despite the differences we see, we are almost exactly identical to each other. We are certainly more identical to each other than to the human selves we were before we came to Earth.

We are all cells of a single Being named *Multiuniversal Self*. When we affirm that all beings, persons and animals, are common threads of one consciousness, we are allowing that every being is fully an extension of the same Divine Mind. We are living wholly in respect, because we realize that each being whom we call a living form represents the same universal power as we do. We no longer believe that our solitary consciousness is superior to any other form of life. We no longer think that our presence makes us better than any other. We understand that a composite of all life forms manifests the reality we live in, and that without each other none of us would exist. When attuning to the Universal Mind, we appreciate that the fragment of consciousness we call self is but one cell in a cosmic Being.

TURNING POINT
IN THE HUMAN STORY

AS THE majority of humanity become filled with the finer appreciation of our individual participations in human evolution, we will open our minds and hearts to being receptive to the overall enhancement of the Divine Presence within us. Our willingness to explore new options and practices in our personal realities is helping us to shape the evolving consensus of opinions and beliefs about the whole. In fact, our personal insights, acted upon in faith and knowing that success is certain, make it possible to alter the course upon which the main body of humanity is moving.

The universe is an integrated Being of many aspects that constitute a whole consciousness. The universe is an integrated Entity that views each of us as a cell of living power that is able to alter the whole in much the same way that the cells of a human body affect the whole body. The universe is affected by every person's indigence, illness, or wellness. The universe is a formless yet living Mind, brought into a comprehensive focus through the anticipations of all its aspects—us. The universe is a free-thinking, synergistic representative of the minds of us all.

We constitute the fabric of existence—by our demeanors, our truth, and our hope. *We* constitute the level of reality that surrounds us—by our visions, our single-mindedness, and our capacity to believe in devotion and bliss.

The universe is composed of our individual abilities to synergize with every other person's desire. The universe is the living expression of the awareness of our Higher Selves, made up of our beliefs and values. The universe is a texturized formlessness of which we are elements, in the same way that the cells of our bodies are elements of the whole beings we are.

Humanity's unfolding consciousness is comparable to the unfolding consciousness of our individual perceptions. There-fore, to heal this world, it is instrumental and powerfully es-sential that we each take responsibility for healing our own soul wounds. As we do, we will heal the wounds of society and heal the wounds of the Consciousness of which *we* are the living voices.

How can we stretch our viewpoints into fresh concepts and ideas and a capacity to be innovative and to conceive new directions? When we identify the estrangements that have separated us and begin to dissolve these through our individ-ual will to live in the light, we begin to remove the barriers that have blocked our spiritual demeanor in the world. We be-gin to unleash the potency of kindness inherent in us. Kind-ness unlocks the door of self-awareness toward which we are drawn.

In the era now before us, we of humanity will find our-selves opening conceptually and living empowered. Our living standard will be the measure of all our choices. Humanity is unfolding synchronistically as each one of us unfolds. Hu-manity is the vision each of us holds and expresses in our deepest understanding. As each one of us expands, so does the whole of the human race exponentially. As each one of us unfolds toward the true Self, so does the whole of the human race exponentially.

Every person is a part of that Being that is the living force. Every one of us represents the consciousness of humanity—by our personal devotion to all that is holy, as we understand it; by our personal dedication to all that is good, as we understand it; and by our synchronicity with the forces of the universe. In whatever way we comprehend it, each of us is reshaping the texture of human life.

Next Level of
The Human Species

THE MIND WITHIN gives us the "Tenets of Clear Being"
to live by, so we can be the persons we were born to be:

- Be in the moment that you are.
- Be exactly where you are.
- Acknowledge your highest level of being.
- Appreciate yourself.
- Appreciate others.
- Exude a clear presence.
- Invoke a clear conscience.
- Honor the highest range of affection.
- Live in the beliefs of goodwill.
- Give of yourself when needed.

The "Tenets of Clear Being" are universal laws of nature.
To register these attributes and be a fully realized human who
kindles inner wisdom and appreciates daily miracles, synthe-
size with your complete essential Self. By accentuating your
whole being, you open your awareness to an upward spiral of
increasing sensitivity. You acquire a cosmic outlook and the
intellect of a seer. You fully develop your ideal Self. You syn-
thesize with your higher Nature. You so sweetly surrender to

your possible being that you embrace your inner truth with grace.

It is possible to be fully actualized while in the present body. To be more of the innate spiritual being you were born to be, wholeheartedly align with your inner Self. Embrace its eternal concepts. Form your fullness by being in sync with the natural order of life and completely in harmony. To manifest your goodness, live as your exponential Self.

Sometimes it seems the human species will never evolve. We certainly do not seem sensitive to our divine Character. Yet by nature all things do evolve. All beings become more than they were. All animals, plants, minerals, even the very atoms of the universe, continually evolve.

We of humanity are very fortunate. We are living during a time of great expansion. Humanity is destined to evolve into a greater breadth of awareness, to become a greater expression of the whole of God, to be in spiritual bodies of consciousness. It is as natural for the human race to ascend in the cosmic spectrum as it is for the amoebae to evolve.

Humanity is on the threshold of a new culture, energizing self-consciousness with a higher altitude, embodying higher aspects of self-reflection. We are living during a time of unparalleled change and we cannot stop this concert of our uniqueness. We cannot hold back our innate power nor delay our higher Stature. All that we are becoming is now unfolding. We are deeded this trust by the God within. Its current is transforming us. Its breath is molding us. Its fuse of hope is inspiring us. Our inner delight is now unfolding.

To embrace this cosmic stretching, to embolden

your inner light and come into the full flower of your true Self, adhere to the "Tenets of Clear Being." Become that point of view, that attitude, that essence. To find the confidence to go on, to hold to your dream and keep your inner flame alive, surrender to the presence of the Divine Consciousness in you. Allow the Mind Force to imbue you. Desire its form in your body, breathe its fire of surrender, and reconstruct your body to its higher dimension—by accepting the wisdom of your soul within you. Accentuate your soul's devotions through your feelings. Liberate your soul's concepts through your intellect. Embrace your soul's kindness through your heart.

Humanity is becoming such a people. We are all babies within a cosmic womb. The placenta is the cosmic awareness of our becoming Selves.

Humanity, the hour is upon us. In due time, we will have fully birthed. In the womb of the Eternal Mother, we are being taught. We are closely linked to that Presence that gives us life. We are infused with its consciousness, alive in its embrace.

We will never become extinct. We will not obliterate ourselves. The Eternal Selves promise that we cannot. They promise that we cannot stop the onward flow. We may resist, but we cannot stop the process of our spiritual evolution.

Today, we are investing in that future world. We are creating the state of our actualized beings, and we are well able. At last, we are moving out of our darkness, releasing our dim sight, breaking free of our old secrets and pains. We are beginning to fathom our potential and to invoke our inner truth: that we are innately good and one with the whole of creation.

As we continue on our present course, increasingly we will access our unique spiritual power. We will discipline ourselves in the arts of self-will and self-love and consciously give of ourselves to this process, because we cannot otherwise be happy with who we are.

Our central attribute as human beings is our ability to stretch. Humanity is now stretching. Soon we will be leaving the womb of the Eternal Mother. Soon we will be newborn beings of light.

Appendix

Healing the Traumas
and Conditions of Your Life

A Workshop

You may wish to tape record this to play it back as a visualization exercise.

First, a brief attunement exercise:

See the blue light within your center.
See the blue light pulsate with your rhythm—
    a living force.

As you inhale:
    See the blue light absorbed into the bloodstream of your body, into the cells of your flesh, purifying your physical body.

As you exhale:
    See dissipating all excretions of imbalance and impurity of the physical body. See yourself releasing all blocks—emotional and physical, attuned to the center of your being.

There is a physical force called ether. This force is substance, and it may be utilized in physical reality in many ways. You may use ether—etheric matter—for vitality, which you breathe in as prana, or blue light.

Etheric force is energy. It may be tapped or utilized. Therefore, let us focus on synchronizing the physical form with the etheric body, bringing these into alignment, so that you feel more complete and more whole.

Realize that the disciplines you practice are a part of this bonding, and that seeking communication with other beings is a form of bonding. Bonding means to unify, to a whole, the many parts that you are.

You are not only your physical form. You are also an etheric body, and many other bodies as well. The reason we are focusing here on the etheric body is to give you substantial information to work with daily. This information is concrete, not abstract. The results will bear immediate fruit, not only in emotional balance, but in manifestation of an ideal, upon which you will focus your attitude.

Let us say that the beginning of synchronizing with the etheric body is to look at attitude. Therefore, allow a thought to come to mind, an area of focus that is meaningful in your life, whether it is a condition or a relationship. Allow an image or a thought form to come to mind.

Notice the emotional feelings you have. Identify and name the various feelings you are experiencing related to the subject.

Now sense your body. Sense your structure. Notice any sensations. Notice any trembling, any vibration. Notice any withdrawal or impact. Notice any kinks or soreness. Now breathe out and release.

The challenge in any degree of reality is letting go. Since that is a state of mind and has nothing to do with the physical form, letting go is a permanent process that is real. Being able to dissipate any wrong (to you) or limiting attitudes is something that will prove useful to you today, tomorrow, and forever.

Now imagine your physical form. See its outline, and see its substance. Become aware of the energy presence of the attitude and thought you have about your subject. See that attitude as a presence or energy force. Observe how it impacts your physical body.

In your mind's eye, as you look both at your form and the energy force of the idea, look at how they work together, how one impacts the other, whether the connection is smooth, natural and dissipated, or whether there are certain conflicts. Simply be aware of these.

Breathe in the blue light, and breathe out all stress, and release.

Now become aware of another body. Superimposed through you and around, a greater body. It looks very similar to the physical body, except that it is not as dense. It is more magnetic. There is more free-flow of vital force through it.

Notice the light and the color of the dense physical body. Then notice the light and the color of the less dense, lighter etheric body. Feel the difference. Observe the difference.

Now look upon the energy force of the idea of your subject. Look at that energy force as a color and a light.

Observe the way in which the subject-idea impacts the physical body. Observe the impact of color and light, and notice the mixture.

At the same time, become aware that the subject-idea is impacting the etheric body. Notice the effect of that energy force on the etheric body. Notice the light and color, any energy patterns, any movement patterns.

Breathe in the blue light, and release.

Now become aware of the energy force of your subject-idea. For a moment, imagine that you are standing beside a cool stream—you, your whole being, here and now who you are. Feel the freshness of nature, of free creative power, the freshness and the release of it on your being. Look into the water, which is very clear, and see your own reflection. Notice how you perceive yourself as you look at your reflection. Notice how you experience who you are—the image. Dip your hands down into that pool and bring up the fresh water and drink it. Think of it as pure substance, pure vital force, which you now take into your being to resupply and nurture the physical body, the etheric body, and the emotional body. As you drink of that vital force, and as you feel it radiate outward through you—synthesizing the various bodies—it is as if one overlaps the other. As you drink in the vital force of life, these bodies meld. They become one—simply extending out endlessly, without any real distinction or separateness.

As you begin to feel more centered and realigned with your natural powers, the attitudes and emotions connected with your subject area are healed through this same change of energy in the body.

As the bodies become one—merged—simply a blend from the inner to the outer, simply a blend from the physical through all the bodies, extensions of the same light, the energy force of the subject is affected in the same manner. Whatever is not in alignment with that blend is dissipated through it, caught up in it and changed along with it, redigested, synergized. So now, when you place the subject-idea out before you and look upon it again—to observe it with a more objective eye—and you see the person or the face of the one who is involved in the situation with you, you begin to realize that attachments are dissolving, needs and extremes are dissolving, and you are flowing as you look upon that face, that condition.

Become aware now of yourself—the whole being, blended—and look out around you at the various disparaging conditions of your life, as if you are on a vast landscape and you are the one thing that is complete and blended; in the way the ocean blends from one color to the next but it is all one, in the way your breath blends with the air around you yet it is all one.

You look upon the conditions around you in your life that do not seem to have the same balance of energy. As you interact with them, you are aware of the separation between you and that subject. You might see that separation as a wall, a wall in the sense that you do not understand the subject and you do not know how to link yourself with it.

Aware now of your whole being blended—the physical, the etheric, and all the other bodies—knowing that you *are* the vital force, that you not only drink it in from life, but you give it out as well in the same way as a flower—give it out now, give out your vital force, send it and wave it through all those conditions that surround you.

Focus in on one in particular, if you wish. Allow the vital force to move through that subject, that condition, that relationship—from your being—and watch the barriers between you and complete integration with the subject-idea disintegrate. The walls disintegrate between you and the idea, the desire, the condition—until you begin to realize that it is simply an extension of you and it is no longer foreign.

When the subject-idea begins to have the same energy

flow and balance as you, it is just as if your body has simply extended that much in that direction. The subject is nothing different or separate from you.

Do that now in circumference, in all directions outward. Simply imagine all disparaging relationships and conditions in your life as energy forces that surround you. Vibrate out the blend of oneness with yourself. Vibrate it out until you begin to see it transform all those energy forces that surround you, until all are complete and you are that much greater and larger than you were. Everything dissipates that is not a part of the blend, until there is nothing left but simply extensions of your bodies, extensions of your being and they are a part of *that* reality.

Being aware of this, bring it back to the present. Think about who you are in this moment. Think about what difference it makes in your feelings toward yourself. Think about what difference it makes in your attitude toward life around you.

Feel what it is like to be open, simply extending the blend of what you are through everything that is called life. *Feel* what it is like to be open.

All right, relax.

The etheric body is your power pack. It is in the etheric body that things first manifest before coming into physical reality. It is in the etheric body that thoughts form, ideas congeal, and conditions are encountered.

When you are so attuned as to introspectively observe your own etheric body, you can discern when something is not in alignment and is not bearing the desired results. You can alter the magnetic properties of that condition in its etheric state by focusing your mind and thought process to the etheric form.

Be aware of altering the magnetic properties of ether, even though subjectively. Be aware of creating matter by first feeling-sensing-perceiving-defining the etheric matter. This is an introspective process that may or may not include psychic perceptions.

When you realize that thought is energy, then you understand that it has a direct affect on ether or etheric matter. Therefore, you can make substantial changes both in your body and in the things you manifest, by working first at the etheric level.

Rather than demand physical results, introspectively discern what is in balance or not in its etheric state. Look at the magnetic polarities. Set up a balance. Then bring it into physical manifestation as a result of your perception.

At this point, go within for a few moments and consider what your etheric body is, how it feels to you, how it is relevant here and now to what you are as a physical person, how it is an extension of what you see you are, how it is the pivot of your force.

This entire workshop was presented to a group
via "channeling" from the Higher Mind

Tenets of Clear Being

- Be in the moment that you are.
- Be exactly where you are.
- Acknowledge your highest level of being.
- Appreciate yourself.
- Appreciate others.
- Exude a clear presence.
- Invoke a clear conscience.
- Honor the highest range of affection.
- Live in the beliefs of goodwill.
- Give of yourself when needed.

RECOMMENDED

Transforming Darkness to Light, Patrisha Richardson
(www.absolutetruthpublication.com, email patrisharich@aol.com)

The Seat of the Soul, Gary Zukav

Freedom in Exile: The Autobiography of the Dalai Lama

Living with Joy, Sanaya Roman

Mastery through Accomplishment, Hazrat Inayat Khan

The Possible Human, Jean Houston

I-Ching Workbook, R. L. Wing

Surfing the Himalayas, Frederick Lenz

The Impersonal Life, DeVorss & Co. Publishers

Pathways to Mastership, audio cassette-tape set by Jonathan Parker, Gateways Institute, P.O. Box 1778, Ojai, California 93023

Chakra Balancing and Energizing, audio cassette by Dick Sutphen, Valley of the Sun Publishing, www.dicksutphen.com

John Gray, Personal Success Seminars

LOOK FOR
CHAROL MESSENGER'S
NEXT BOOKS

PETALS OF SELF-DISCOVERY
A personal guide for living the soul path
With workbook for awakening your soul power

HIGHER SELF INITIATION
A step-by-step action plan for higher self integration
The daily routine for being your higher self now

WINGS OF LIGHT
Angels in our everyday lives
How to communicate with your angels

VISIONS OF SERENDIPITY
Orders of the Angels
The Angels' Obligations to Humanity

INCARNATION OF ANGELS
How Many of Us Got Here
Levels of Existence—From Here to the I Am

THE NEW EARTH
The Order of the Universe
The Magical Kingdom
The Fifth Dimension

COMMUNICATING WITH YOUR HIGHER SELF

HOW TO CHANNEL AND WRITE
FROM YOUR HIGHER SELF

And more!

Revealed Teachings